Moving Images

The experience of watching films – entertaining, moving, instructive, frightening or exciting as they may be – can be enriched by the opportunity to reflect upon them from unconventional perspectives. *Moving Images: Psychoanalytic reflections on film* offers its readers one such viewpoint in accessible language, informed by Andrea Sabbadini's psychoanalytic insights and therapeutic experience. Using a psychoanalytic interpretative approach, twenty-five important feature films are discussed as the artistic vehicles of new, unsuspected meanings.

The first chapter looks at films that represent psychoanalytic work itself, with therapists and their patients as their main characters. The remaining five chapters cover movies on themes of central concern to analytic theorists and clinicians, such as childhood and adolescent development, and varieties of intimate relationships among adults, including: romantic love and its disturbing association to death fantasies; eroticism and prostitution; and voyeuristic desire (a significant phenomenon in this context given its parallels with the activity of watching films). Andrea Sabbadini's psychoanalytic approach, which explores the part played by unconscious factors in shaping the personality and behaviour of film characters, is used to interpret their internal world and the emotional conflicts engendered by the vicissitudes they live through. The book is completed by a filmography and biographical notes on film directors.

Moving Images presents the relationship between cinema and psychoanalysis as a complex one. These two most different of cultural phenomena are shown to share a wish on the part of their practitioners to uncover profound truths about the human condition, and to provide a language with which to describe them. Going beyond futile psycho-historical attempts to analyze filmmakers through their products, or a superficial application of psychoanalytic concepts to film, Sabbadini shows how both cinema and psychoanalysis can benefit from a meaningful interdisciplinary dialogue between them. The book will be of special interest to practising psychoanalysts and students, scholars and historians of film studies.

Andrea Sabbadini is a Fellow of the British Psychoanalytical Society and its Director of Publications. He works in private practice in London, is the director of the European Psychoanalytic Film Festival, and is also the film section editor of the *International Journal of Psychoanalysis*. His edited books include *Even Paranoids Have Enemies* (Routledge 1998), *The Couch and the Silver Screen* (Routledge 2003) and *Projected Shadows* (Routledge 2007).

The New Library of Psychoanalysis

General Editor: Alessandra Lemma

The New Library of Psychoanalysis was launched in 1987 in association with the Institute of Psychoanalysis, London. It took over from the International Psychoanalytical Library which published many of the early translations of the works of Freud and the writings of most of the leading British and Continental psychoanalysts.

The purpose of the New Library of Psychoanalysis is to facilitate a greater and more widespread appreciation of psychoanalysis and to provide a forum for increasing mutual understanding between psychoanalysts and those working in other disciplines such as the social sciences, medicine, philosophy, history, linguistics, literature and the arts. It aims to represent different trends both in British psychoanalysis and in psychoanalysis generally. The New Library of Psychoanalysis is well placed to make psychoanalytic writings from other European countries available to the English-speaking world, and to increase the interchange of ideas between British and American psychoanalysts. Through the Teaching Series, the New Library of Psychoanalysis now also publishes books that provide comprehensive, yet accessible, overviews of selected subject areas aimed at those studying psychoanalysis and those involved with fields related to psychoanalysis, such as the social sciences, philosophy, literature and the arts.

The Institute of Psychoanalysis, together with the British Psychoanalytical Society, runs a low-fee psychoanalytic clinic, organizes lectures and scientific events concerned with psychoanalysis and publishes the *International Journal of Psychoanalysis*. It runs a training course in psychoanalysis which leads to membership of the International Psychoanalytical Association – the body which preserves internationally accepted standards of training, professional entry, and professional ethics and practice for psychoanalysis (as initiated and developed by Sigmund Freud). Distinguished members of the institute have included Michael Balint, Wilfred Bion, Ronald Fairbairn, Anna Freud, Ernest Jones, Melanie Klein, John Rickman and Donald Winnicott.

Previous general editors have included David Tuckett, who played a very active role in the establishment of the New Library. He was followed as general editor by Elizabeth Bott Spillius, who was in turn followed by Susan Budd and then by Dana Birksted-Breen.

Current members of the Advisory Board include Liz Allison, Giovanna di Ceglie, Rosemary Davies and Richard Rusbridger.

Previous members of the Advisory Board include Christopher Bollas, Ronald Britton, Catalina Bronstein, Donald Campbell, Sara Flanders, Stephen Grosz, John Keene, Eglé Laufer, Alessandra Lemma, Juliet Mitchell, Michael Parsons, Rosine Jozef Perelberg, Mary Target and David Taylor.

Mind Works: Techniques and Creativity in Psychoanalysis Antonino Ferro
Doubt Conviction and the Analytic Process: Selected Papers of Michael Feldman Michael
Feldman
Melanie Klein in Berlin: Her First Psychoanalyses of Children Claudia Frank
The Psychotic Wavelength: A Psychoanalytic Perspective for Psychiatry Richard Lucas
Betweenity: A Discussion of the Concept of Borderline Judy Gammelgaard
The Intimate Room: Theory and Technique of the Analytic Field Giuseppe Civitarese
Bion Today Edited by Chris Mawson
Secret Passages: The Theory and Technique of Interpsychic Relations Stefano Bolognini
*Intersubjective Processes and the Unconscious: An Integration of Freudian, Kleinian and Bionian
Perspectives* Lawrence J. Brown
Seeing and Being Seen: Emerging from a Psychic Retreat John Steiner
Avoiding Emotions, Living Emotions Antonio Ferro
Projective Identification: The Fate of a Concept Edited by Elizabeth Spillius and Edna
O'Shaughnessy
Creative Readings: Essays on Seminal Analytic Works Thomas Ogden
The Maternal Lineage Edited by Paola Mariotti
Donald Winnicott Today Edited by Jan Abram
Symbiosis and Ambiguity: A Psychoanalytic Study Edited by John Churcher, José Bleger and
Leopoldo Bleger
Psychotic Temptation Liliane Abensour
Supervision in Psychoanalysis: The Sao Paulo Seminars Antonino Ferro
Transference and Countertransference Today Robert Oelsner

TITLES IN THE NEW LIBRARY OF PSYCHOANALYSIS
TEACHING SERIES

Reading Freud: A Chronological Exploration of Freud's Writings Jean-Michel Quinodoz
Listening to Hanna Segal: Her Contribution to Psychoanalysis Jean-Michel Quinodoz
Reading French Psychoanalysis Edited by Dana Birksted-Breen, Sara Flanders and Alain
Gibeault
Reading Winnicott Lesley Caldwell and Angela Joyce
Initiating Psychoanalysis: Perspectives Bernard Reith, Sven Lagerlöf, Penelope Crick, Mette
Møller and Elisabeth Skale
Infant Observation Frances Salo and Nick Midgley

TITLES IN THE NEW LIBRARY OF PSYCHOANALYSIS
'BEYOND THE COUCH' SERIES

Under the Skin: A Psychoanalytic Study of Body Modification Alessandra Lemma
Engaging with Climate Change: Psychoanalytic and Interdisciplinary Perspectives Edited by
Sally Weintrobe
Research on the Couch: Single Case Studies, Subjectivity, and Psychoanalytic Knowledge
R.D. Hinshelwood
Psychoanalysis in the Technoculture Era Edited by Alessandra Lemma and
Luigi Caparrotta
Moving Images: Psychoanalytic Reflections on Film Andrea Sabbadini

Moving Images

Psychoanalytic reflections on film

Andrea Sabbadini

Routledge
Taylor & Francis Group

LONDON AND NEW YORK

First published 2014
by Routledge
27 Church Road, Hove, East Sussex, BN3 2FA

and by Routledge
711 Third Avenue, New York, NY 10017

Routledge is an imprint of the Taylor & Francis Group, an informa business

British Library Cataloguing-in-Publication Data

A catalogue record for this book is available from the British Library

Library of Congress Cataloging-in-Publication Data

Sabbadini, Andrea.
Moving images : psychoanalytic reflections on film / Andrea Sabbadini.
    pages cm
  Includes bibliographical references.
  1. Psychoanalysis and motion pictures.   2. Psychiatry in motion pictures.   3. Motion pictures—Psychological aspects.   I. Title.
    PN1995.9.P783S24   2014
    791.4301'9—dc23   2013034300

ISBN: 978-0-415-73611-4 (hbk)
ISBN: 978-0-415-73612-1 (pbk)
ISBN: 978-1-315-81498-8 (ebk)

Typeset in Times
by Apex CoVantage, LLC

MIX
Paper from
responsible sources
FSC   FSC® C013056
www.fsc.org

Printed and bound in Great Britain by
TJ International Ltd, Padstow, Cornwall

To Leo and Sam

Contents

Acknowledgements

Parts of this book contain passages taken from articles originally published elsewhere, or are revised versions of them, as from the following list. My gratitude goes to the editors and publishers who have generously granted their permission to use them here.

THE INTERNATIONAL JOURNAL OF PSYCHOANALYSIS AND WILEY

Letters, words and metaphors: A psychoanalytic reading of Michael Radford's *Il Postino*. *IJP*, 79(3): 609–611, 1998.

Watching voyeurs: Michael Powell's *Peeping Tom* (1960). *IJP*, 81(4): 809–813, 2000.

'Not something destroyed but something that is still alive': *Amores Perros* at the intersection of rescue fantasies. *IJP*, 84(3): 755–764, 2003.

Between physical desire and emotional involvement. Reflections on Fréderic Fonteyne's film *Une Liaison Pornographique*. *IJP*, 90(6): 1441–1447, 2009.

THE BRITISH JOURNAL OF PSYCHOTHERAPY AND BLACKWELL PUBLISHING

The attraction of fear: Some psychoanalytic observations on Alfred Hitchcock's *Vertigo*. *BJP*, 16(4): 507–511, 2000.

Psychoanalysis and its (mis)representations in films: From Pabst, Hitchcock and Huston to Brody's *Nineteen Nineteen*. *BJP*, 18(3): 433–439, 2002.

PALGRAVE MACMILLAN

Of boxes, peepholes and other perverse objects. A psychoanalytic look at Luis Buñuel's *Belle de Jour*. In P.W. Evans and I. Santaolalla (Eds.), *Luis Buñuel. New Readings*. London: BFI Publishing, 2004, pp. 117–127.

PSICANÁLISE EM REVISTA

Encurralados na Cidade sem Deus. *Psicanálise em Revista*, 5(1): 111–117, 2007.

SOVREMENNIK

Cinema and psychoanalysis. *Sovremennik*, 2, 2011, pp. 320–332.

PHOTOGRAPHS APPEAR BY COURTESY OF THE FOLLOWING ORGANIZATIONS:

Neumann-Filmproduktion (*Geheimnesse einer Seele*); Selznick International Pictures (*Spellbound*); BFI, Channel Four and Hugh Brody (*Nineteen Nineteen*); Cecchi Gori Pictures (*Il Postino*); Dino de Laurentiis Cinematografica (*Le Notti di Cabiria*); Memfis Film (*Lilya-4-Ever*); Robert et Raymond Hakim (*Belle de Jour*); Kestrel Films Ltd. (*Kes*); Elías Querejeta Producciones Cinematográficas S.L. (*El Espiritu de la Colmena* and *Cria Cuervos*); Estudios Picasso (*El Laberinto del Fauno*); Tevere Film (*Germania Anno Zero*); Wingnut Films (*Heavenly Creatures*); O2 Filmes (*Cidade de Deus*); Kirov Consult (*Mila ot Mars*); ARP Sélection (*Une Liaison pornographique*); Altavista Films (*Amores Perros*); Les Films de la Boétie (*Le Boucher*); Compañia Iberoamericana de TV (*Matador*); Paramount Pictures (*Vertigo* and *Rear Window*); Zespol Filmowy 'Tor' (*Krotki Film O Milosci*); Clasa Films Mundiales (*Homework*); Michael Powell Theatre (*Peeping Tom*).

Introduction

Cinema and psychoanalysis may appear to be an odd couple. What could an artistic medium mostly engaged in the representation of fictional stories, and a psychological discipline committed to the understanding of the deeper recesses of the human mind, possibly have to say to each other?

Since early on in their relatively brief history, however, psychoanalysts, filmmakers and film scholars have on many occasions, and in a variety of different ways, attempted to communicate, interact or influence one another. Often they have reaped rewarding results. For instance, it is a common occurrence that the clinical work (as well as the personal life) of many psychoanalysts is affected by what they watch on the screen. Viewing movies, then, may offer them a new perspective on the material their patients bring to their sessions. They also gain opportunity to further reflect on their experiences and, in the process, to gain a richer understanding of their internal world.

Psychoanalysts, beginning with Otto Rank back in 1914,[1] have often expressed much interest about the world of cinema. As a result, over the past few decades psychoanalysis has provided, with the help of its methodology and conceptual tools, a valuable contribution to film criticism, commenting on film's narratives and characters, its structure and technical features, its cultural significance and its spectatorship reception. Indeed, the main body of psychoanalytic writings on cinema consists of the interpretation of individual movies through a variety of theoretical ideas familiar to analysts from their clinical work. Depending on their own orientation, those psychoanalysts discussing film and writing about it have made reference to such concepts as the Oedipus Complex, Castration Anxiety, Archetypes, the Symbolic Order, the Paranoid-schizoid Position, the Transitional Space of creativity, and so forth. Mostly concerned as they are with a detailed analysis of the unconscious aspects of characters and their stories, these texts enrich film theory with original and often controversial interpretations.[2]

Another relevant observation in this context is that, as many of us know, the recounting of the experience of going to the movies and the cognitive and emotional impact that films have on their spectators could fill much psychoanalytic session time. Analysands often make references to films; their dreams and waking-life fantasies are coloured by what they have watched on the big or small screen; their frequent identifications are with movie stars or with the characters these actors play in front of the camera.

On their part, many filmmakers wishing to sharpen their artistic eye frequently engage, more or less deliberately, with psychoanalytic ideas. They have found these ideas helpful in their construction of three-dimensional, truer-to-reality characters and psychologically credible plots. Since the early days of cinema many films have drawn their inspiration from issues they share with the analysts: their structure and language may reflect the Unconscious as studied by psychoanalysis, and they present characters with the kinds of problems or psychopathologies familiar to analytic practitioners. Some even attempt to represent the psychoanalytic profession itself (See Chapter One). Some filmmakers, especially in the Hollywood scene of the 1950s and 1960s when our profession enjoyed much popularity in films, had been themselves in analysis and had then translated onto the screen their personal experience of it (sometimes, it must be said, rather clumsily). These days psychoanalysts and filmmakers find opportunities to engage in constructive dialogues, thus enriching their respective disciplines through a creative process of cross-fertilization.

While a "psychoanalytic cinema" as a discrete genre does not exist, some films seem to be particularly suitable for psychoanalytic readings, and are in turn more likely to provide therapists with observations and insights useful in their clinical work. These are movies which would present their characters in an explicitly psychological way, with emphasis on their inner world and personality; they may be represented in their ambivalent or conflictual aspects, their past history may be taken into account and even their unconscious motivations explored, thus allowing spectators to identify with them, rather than idealize or denigrate them as they would with more superficial portraits of heroes and villains, cops and robbers, or cowboys and Indians. Other films may have a special appeal to psychoanalytic audiences not so much for their content but because their language is suggestive of the free-associative mode of expression, or because they encourage a sort of free-floating attention in order to be appreciated, or because of a certain oneiric atmosphere pervading them. By portraying psychologically recognizable characters, engaging in intelligent and sensitive dialogues and interactions, and being more concerned with subtleties of emotional and interpersonal experiences than with dramatic plots or the display of special effects, such movies can enrich our knowledge of various aspects of our existence, both in its normal and psychopathological manifestations. Sometimes they usefully remind us of how unclear the boundaries can be between the normal and the pathological.

What does a psychoanalyst like myself do when he goes *beyond the couch*? Among a number of other occupations, he watches films, perhaps on a DVD in front of his laptop, or on an old video played on the small screen, or (better) sitting in a comfortable armchair in a cinema.

Many people watch film simply because they wish to be entertained, or because they want to learn about the world (or about themselves), or because they are looking for something to excite them, to scare them, to lift them up from their

depression, or to calm them down from their state of agitation. All of these motivations may, at different times, apply to myself too. However, the point is that for
me watching a film – pleasant, entertaining, educational, uplifting, reassuring as
it may well be – is not enough. Not enough, that is, unless I can also find the time
and space to *reflect* on the experience: to think about it by myself, to discuss it
with trusted friends or colleagues, to read about it and, occasionally, also to write
down my impressions of it.

The latter is what I have been doing with the films included in this volume. I
had already presented some of these thoughts to mixed audiences in various cin-
emas in London and elsewhere, some to filmmakers or other psychoanalysts in
the context of international conferences, or at the *European Psychoanalytic Film
Festival* which I have been directing since 2001. Some have already been out in
print in professional journals or as book chapters. Collecting them here now and
making them available to a wider readership makes me feel a mixture of pride
and humility. The pride has to do with that modicum of narcissistic gratification
which I consider a healthy component of our lives, and without which none of us
would feel motivated to achieve much at all beyond just trying to keep alive. The
humility, on the other hand, concerns my awareness that with this book I will not
be providing a systematic, scholarly approach to film criticism, nor will I offer
any new general theoretical model for the interpretation of films, nor will I necessarily be contributing, by focusing on the structure and content of movies, to a
better understanding of psychoanalytic models of the mind.

What I ultimately try to do here is share with the readers my reflections, pre-
dominantly (though not exclusively) informed by psychoanalytic knowledge and
experience, about a small number of the many movies which have enriched my
understanding of human beings. I said "not exclusively" because, contrary to
a rather grandiose belief held by some of my colleagues, there are aspects of
the lived lives which we hear about in our consulting rooms and of the filmed
films which we watch when we go beyond the couch that are not easily amenable
(alas!) to psychoanalytic interpretations.

If my intention, then, is to offer here a set of readings of films from a psychoanalytic perspective, in the process of doing so I would also be using films in
order to illustrate a number of psychoanalytic ideas and to convey a sense of what
analytic work consists of. (Others might be using, say, novels or fairy-tales, not to
mention case studies or vignettes from their clinical work with patients.) In fact
I think there is a complementarity between these aims, and that by oscillating as
I will be doing between these different registers, both tasks could be pursued at
the same time. Ultimately it is not a question of prioritizing the potential value
of cinema for psychoanalysis, or of psychoanalysis for cinema, but to preserve
a creative tension between these two approaches without imposing an artificial
resolution upon them.

Cinema and psychoanalysis are of interest to each other primarily because of
the many thematic affinities between them and because some of the characters
we meet on the screen may have uncanny resemblance with those we are familiar

with from psychoanalytic work. However, those who, like myself, try to explore the connections between these two cultural areas are not just intrigued by such similarities in the objects (or subjects) that filmmakers and analysts deal with. Nor are we just fascinated to discover some of the remarkable affinities in the more creative aspects of their work, such as through the process (of crucial importance to both) of editing the material available to them; nor by the fact that, as Glen Gabbard has pointed out, "to a large extent, film speaks the language of the unconscious" (1997, p. 429).

What I think provides the deeper stimulus to our interest in this field is a sort of fundamental *curiosity* about the human condition. Psychologists will attribute this curiosity to our innate need to explore and find out about the world that surrounds us ("epistemophilic drive," they call it). Meanwhile, psychoanalysts will relate it to the process of sublimation, whereby unconscious sexual and aggressive energies are channeled into such socially acceptable endeavours as scientific research or creative activities. What matters here is that we know that this curiosity gets rewarded again and again by the "visual pleasures" (to borrow from the title of Laura Mulvey's seminal paper [1975]) that good cinema donates to its spectators, combined with the (mostly) auditory pleasures that we obtain from psychoanalytic work. It is this healthy (as opposed to morbidly voyeuristic – see Chapter Six) curiosity about human beings and the countless variations in their vicissitudes, as well as the insights and surprises that both cinema and psychoanalysis reserve for us, that constitute the intellectual and the emotional motivation to our research into their connections.

The choice of films either presented in detail or just referred to here is arbitrary and does not have much respect for historical considerations; the works discussed in this book, mostly produced in the last half-century, are not ordered chronologically. Nor do my choices reflect geographical consideration (though most of them come from European countries). As readers of this book will not fail to notice, I may have left out works that would have deserved to be included, either because I was unaware of their relevance or even existence, or because of my own taste or bias. Here I can only hide behind the good-enough reason that *De gustibus disputandum non est* ("One can't disagree with someone else's taste").

However, if my choice of individual works is idiosyncratic, this material is organized in a coherent fashion within what I hope will prove to be a solid enough underlying structure. My intention here was clear: to select some of the main psychoanalytic themes that have occupied our discipline since its early days (which, incidentally, coincide with those of cinema: Freud and Breuer's *Studies on Hysteria* were published in 1895, the same year when the Lumière brothers screened their first movies), and then to introduce films that would illustrate those issues.

These include cinematic reflections on psychoanalysis itself, with movies telling stories whose protagonists are analysts and their patients (Chapter One: *A young profession*) in antithesis, or perhaps complementarity, with Chapter Two (. . . *and the oldest one*) about prostitution; Chapters Three (*The young ones*) and Four (. . . *and slightly older ones*) look at child and adolescent development, as illustrated by films with young people as their main characters; Chapter Five (*Between eros and thanatos*) scratches the surface on love as portrayed in some of its infinite variations on the screen, including its disturbing association with death; and finally, focusing on one such variation, Chapter Six (*Watching voyeurs*) will consider how cinema attempts to reflect upon itself, insofar as film is an object of our visual curiosity.

I have provided enough information about each movie's narrative and characters to allow even readers who have never watched them to follow my comments. Most of these films are on the market in DVD format, and trailers and clips from them are freely available on such websites as YouTube. Please note that I shall refer to all films in the text by their English titles, with a few exceptions – *Il Postino* (The Postman), *Cría Cuervos* (Raise Ravens), *Ossessione* (Obsession), *Amores Perros* (Love Is a Bitch) and *Le Boucher* (The Butcher). The titles of these films are better known in Anglophone countries in their original languages.

These six chapters are followed by an appendix with brief biographical notes about the directors of the main films being presented, a filmography of the movies mentioned or discussed, and a glossary of psychoanalytic terms.

Notes

1. He wrote one century ago: "The uniqueness of cinematography in visibly portraying psychological events calls our attention, with exaggerated clarity, to the fact that the interesting and meaningful problems of man's relation to himself – and the fateful disturbance of this relation – finds here an imaginative representation" (Rank 1914, p. 7).
2. It must be noted here that those "psycho-historical" studies speculating on the personality or pathology of the filmmakers themselves, as revealed by treating their works as if they were symptoms, may have enjoyed some popularity in the past. However, these studies now tend to be discredited as having little in common with more serious psychoanalytic approaches.

Chapter 1

A young profession

Films on psychoanalysis

The films considered in this first chapter, by featuring as their main characters analysts and/or their patients (with one exception, as I will explain), attempt to represent – but often end up *mis*-representing – psychoanalysis itself. In these movies our profession is sometimes presented in the dramatically effective but inaccurate version of the therapist being engaged in the recovery of repressed traumas for the explanation of current events, with much use of flashbacks (the filmic equivalent of memory). This approach has been exploited, for instance, in some of Alfred Hitchcock's movies, such as *Spellbound* (1945) and *Marnie* (1964). *Spellbound* is also an example of the way in which psychoanalysis is often misrepresented in cinema by showing analysts acting out their (counter-transference) love for their analysands as they get involved in romantic or sexual activities with each other. An exception to this caricaturization can be found in the television series *In Treatment* (2010) in which the character of the psychotherapist (played by Gabriel Byrne) is shown as emotionally vulnerable to the seductive temptations of one of his patients, but professional enough to resist enacting his erotic feelings for her.[1]

Another distorted picture of our profession on the screen concerns the suggestion, to comical effect, that analysts are more insane than their patients (*Deconstructing Harry*, Allen 1997). Other times analysts are portrayed as naive, unprofessional, greedy, abusive, or even involved in criminal activities. Freud may have been right in his letter of 9 June 1925 to Karl Abraham, who had invited him to collaborate on the first film project ever made about psychoanalysis, *Secrets of a Soul* (Pabst 1926). Freud replied: "I do not believe that satisfactory plastic representation of our abstractions is at all possible" (Abraham and Freud 1965, p. 547).

Films which represent the psychoanalytic profession may have as their main characters a psychoanalyst (*The Son's Room*, Moretti 2001), Freud himself (*Freud: The Secret Passion,* Huston 1962), psychoanalytic patients (*Nineteen Nineteen*, Brody 1985), or both analyst and analysand (*Secrets of a Soul*, Pabst 1926; *My Own Executioner*, Kimmins 1948; *Inconscientes*, Oristrell 2004). Not surprisingly, prominent patients involved in scandalous relationships have attracted special attention from filmmakers – at least three of them in Sabina Spielrein's case: *My Name Was Sabina Spielrein* (Màrton 2002), *The Soul Keeper* (Faenza 2003), and *A Dangerous Method* (Cronenberg 2011).

The earliest example of something approaching the presence of psychoanalysis in a film can be found in *The Mystery of the Rocks of Kador* by French director Léonce Perret (1912). In this film, "a celebrated foreign alienist physician" saves the heroine Suzanne from madness by utilizing the "luminous vibrations of cinematographic images" to induce in her a hypnotic state leading to psychotherapeutic suggestion (see Bergstrom 1999, pp. 15–20). However, the first serious filmic representation of psychoanalysis is the German feature *Secrets of a Soul* (Pabst 1926), while psychoanalysis only reached Hollywood in the 1940s with Hitchcock's *Spellbound* (1945).

Freud was reserved about his personal life, sceptical about biographies of any kind, and unsympathetic to the medium of cinema. He only reluctantly agreed to be filmed in 1928 by one of his American patients, Philip R. Lehman, for a documentary that was also to include shots of many other prominent psychoanalysts. Its final fifty-minute (!) version, entitled *Sigmund Freud: His Family and Colleagues, 1928–1947*, was edited, restored and completed by Lehman's daughter Lynne Lehman Weiner and released in 1985 (Marinelli 2004). However, Freud would have thought of a feature film about himself – such as John Huston's *Freud. The Secret Passion* (1962) – anathema. This movie, though, turned out to be no conventional Hollywood biopic as it is concerned not so much with Freud-the-man but with a subject matter that we know to be fundamentally resistant to representation: the Unconscious itself. Making this movie caused drama among Huston, Universal Pictures, Huston's first screenwriter (no less than the French existentialist philosopher Jean-Paul Sartre), and the film's eponymous star, a sensitive if also disturbed Montgomery Clift. The film concentrates on the early years of psychoanalysis, from 1885 to Freud's father's death in 1896 and the publication at the turn of the century of *The Interpretation of Dreams* (1900). Crucial to those years are the discovery and then the abandonment (circa 1897) of the so-called seduction theory of psychoneurosis, which provide the theoretical underpinnings to the movie's narrative. Freud's patient in the film, Cecily (Susannah York), a composite of the published case histories of Anna O., Dora and others, is affected by severe hysterical symptoms eventually understood by Freud in relation to her childhood's Oedipal fantasies. Or should I say traumata? It is remarkable that Freud's abandonment, more than a century ago, of the seduction theory should still today cause heated arguments about psychoanalysis. Seduction or abuse? The emphasis has moved, with the words, from a view of the child colluding (i.e. playing some role in the event, however ambiguously defined) to that of the child being a passive victim. Far beyond semantics, this dilemma seems often unresolvable, for it concerns the impossibility of differentiating the relative effects of psychological and external reality – fantasy from history. In Huston's film, Freud and Cecily embark upon a journey towards self-knowledge, with an insistence on the imagery of light and darkness emphasizing the arduous character of such a quest.

It must be noticed here that one of the problems concerning many of the representations of our psychoanalytic profession on the screen is a certain confusion, especially in the minds of Hollywood filmmakers and their audiences, between psychoanalysis and psychiatry.[2] Such confusion is at least in part justified by the fact that until not long ago all American psychoanalysts were also psychiatrists. It is a small but significant detail that psychiatrists display portraits of Freud on their walls in such important films about mental institutions as Litvak's *The Snake Pit* (1948), Johnson's *The Three Faces of Eve* (1957) and Fuller's *Shock Corridor* (1963), a group of films that also includes Forman's popular *One Flew Over the Cuckoo's Nest* (1975).

*****

Secrets of a Soul[3] by Georg Wilhelm Pabst was completed in 1926. Through this experimental project backed by the powerful Berlin UFA film company, producer and co-screenwriter Hans Neumann intended to present psychoanalysis to the general public in a scientifically correct, but also visually engaging form. Two leading analysts of the time agreed to act as consultants for this project: then-president of the International Psychoanalytical Association Karl Abraham, who died three months before the film opened, and his *Berlin Poliklinik* colleague Hanns Sachs. They provided clear enough guidelines to allow Pabst, one of the major film directors of the Weimar generation, to produce not quite the *Lehrfilm* (educational documentary) that Neumann and Abraham had originally intended, but an attractive and thought-provoking account of psychoanalysis. It was the first and arguably one of the most successful attempts of this kind to date.[4]

We cannot be certain about Freud's reasons for dissociating himself from this well-meaning project – an attitude which Friedberg calls "a reaction-formation of defense and suspicion" (Friedberg 1990, p. 41). After all, for the sake of making psychoanalytic ideas more widely available, in those same years Freud had been prepared to write entries for the *Encyclopaedia Britannica* (Freud 1923) and "An Autobiographical Study" (Freud 1925b). As mentioned above, he wrote to Abraham that he did not believe that psychoanalysis could be represented in film. However, as Friedberg points out, Freud himself had been looking for "topological metaphors to describe and make more tangible the otherwise abstract concept of the unconscious" (Friedberg 1990, p. 44), as is clear from his own paper *A Note upon the "Mystic Writing Pad"* (Freud 1925a).

Furthermore, there is a rare and remarkable reference to cinema in a letter Freud wrote from Rome to his family as early as 22 September 1907. Its relevant section is worth quoting:

On the Piazza Colonna behind which I am staying, as you know, several thousand people congregate every night. . . . [O]n the roof of a house at the other end of the piazza there is a screen on which a *società Italiana* projects lantern slides *(fotoreclami)*. They are actually advertisements, but to beguile the public these are interspersed with pictures of landscapes, Negroes of the

Congo, glacier ascents, and so on. But since these wouldn't be enough, the boredom is interrupted by short cinematographic performances for the sake of which the old children (your father included) suffer quietly the advertisements and monotonous photographs. They are stingy with these tidbits, however, so I have had to look at the same thing over and over again. When I turn to go I detect a certain tension in the crowd, which makes me look again, and sure enough a new performance has begun, and so I stay on. Until 9 P.M. I usually remain spellbound; then I begin to feel too lonely in the crowd, so I return to my room to write to you all after having ordered a bottle of fresh water. The others who promenade in couples or *undici, dodici* stay on as long as the music and lantern slides last.

(in E. L. Freud 1961, pp. 261–262).

What Freud says in this letter promises a future fascination for the new art form; however, not only did he not believe that psychoanalytic ideas could be represented by cinema but, for the rest of his life, he displayed as little interest in films as he had in some other artistic disciplines such as music. "Filmmaking can be avoided as little as – so it seems – bobbed hair," Freud wrote in a letter to Sándor Ferenczi on 14 August 1925, "but I myself won't get mine cut, and don't intend to be brought into personal connection with any film" (in Falzeder and Brabant 2000, p. 222).

In the above-quoted letter to Abraham, Freud had added about *Secrets of a Soul*: "I would much prefer if my name did not have anything to do with it at all,"[5] but he must have known that this would not be possible. On 26 July 1926 the *New York Times* claimed that Freud himself was going to direct the film! We are also intrigued today by the "good deal of consternation" (Jones 1957, p. 121) this good movie has apparently attracted from the psychoanalytic establishment as a whole, in spite of its commercial and critical success and the fact that it is difficult to imagine what there is in *Secrets of a Soul* to which psychoanalysts of the time could have objected. But then most of the attacks on the film came from those who apparently had not even seen it. There is no question that "faced with the choice of *either* popularising psychoanalysis properly *or* risking being damned for not having done so, Abraham and Sachs decided to do that which they considered would best serve the Cause" (Ries 1995, p. 767).

Pabst's achievement here is impressive as he manages to put forward a detailed, accurate and respectful fictional account, with the structure of a detective story, of the psychoanalytic case of a middle-aged neurotic chemist. We watch Martin Fellman (Werner Krauss) becoming extremely jealous when he hears that a younger man (i.e. his wife's cousin and his own childhood friend), will be visiting them soon. His madness, revealed in the film both in his behaviour and in a dream (at ten full minutes, one of the longest in the history of cinema), takes the form of a phobia of knives, razors and other blades, which he feels compelled to use destructively against his wife. A not-too-coincidental encounter with psychoanalyst Dr Orth (played by the Russian actor Pavel Pavlov), to whom he will freely reveal his feelings as well as recount his frightening dream, will resolve his psychopathology.[6]

The lead role is played by that famous actor Werner Krauss, who had been the *Döppelganger* mad psychiatrist in the horror Expressionist masterpiece *The Cabinet of Dr Caligari* (Wiene 1920). Not an easy task, also considering the paradox that this is a *silent* film about the *talking* cure. This, though, is perhaps also one of its assets: because the film is silent, we the viewers, who are only given minimum help by a few inter-titles, have to make a more creative use of our own imagination in order to understand the movie's complexities. Compare this stylish effort with the vulgar caricatures of our profession in so many Hollywood movies of the 1950s and 1960s, where analysts take masses of useless notes during sessions, flood their patients with superficial interpretations, and frequently end up on the couch with them.[7]

Secrets of a Soul belongs to that intermediate æsthetic territory that could be located between the claustrophobic theatrical worlds of Expressionism and *Kammerspiel*, and the emergence of the *Neue Sachlichkeit* (New Objectivity) of Pabst's best works, such as *The Joyless Street* (1925) and *Pandora's Box* (1928). In these we see a "veristic" approach that was to evolve during the Second World War into the Italian *Neorealismo*.[8] The Expressionistic component of the film is evident in its manneristic use of symbolism. In his critical appraisal of Pabst, described as an ambiguous figure with an extraterritorial career, Rentschler noticed that "blades sever links and create new boundaries. Mirrors, likewise, fix identities and confound the self. It is fitting that Pabst's early study of male anxiety, *Secrets of a Soul*, introduces both props into the opening sequence as pliers of uncertainty" (Rentschler 1990, pp. 2–3). Other symbolically loaded objects are prominent (a phallic tower, a key, a doll), especially in the dream sequence where we also find a number of special effects, such as superimpositions and reverse motion, to represent the mechanisms of condensation and displacement of the dream-work.

It is interesting to note that the dream images, which have a dark background when first used to illustrate the progression of Martin Fellman's psychopathology, are then repeated with a whitened background when the dream is reported to the analyst. Then the analyst as *Deus ex machina* provides the interpretations that will pave the Royal Road to the resolution of our chemist's problems. Symbolism, we may notice, was also a trademark of the Surrealist movement that in those same years was producing other analysis-inspired films, such as Luis Buñuel's *Un Chien Andalou* (1928) and *L'Age d'Or* (1930).[9]

In *Secrets of a Soul* Pabst presents a variety of themes intended to introduce his audience to a psychoanalytic understanding of mental processes and phenomena and to their peculiar idiom, of which I can only mention here a few instances. The defensive mechanism of *denial* is illustrated by Martin Fellman throwing into the fire the newspaper reporting a murder that had taken place down the road (i.e. his own unconsciously wished-for uxoricide). Leaving his front-door key at the restaurant, which will be picked up by the psychoanalyst who will then be offering him his services, is an effective reference to everyday-life *parapraxes*, while the little girl who comes to his laboratory and the dogs he keeps at home are all instances of the *displacement* of his conflictual wish to have children – something impossible at the time as his symptoms included sexual impotence. Under stress, our chemist gives into *regression* and is only too pleased to allow his mother to mince his meal up for him as if he were a young child. Pabst enhanced his audience's understanding with a glossy program sold at the theatre door and an introductory booklet written for the occasion by Hans Sachs himself (1926).

Martin Fellman's worries about razors put him simultaneously into the safe hands of the barber and those of the psychoanalyst. The latter waits before uttering his interpretations and allows his analysand to get involved in the therapeutic process before recommending that he lie on the couch. Filmed in flashback, the childhood scene, central to the patient's neurosis as well as to the dénouement in the film, is psychologically convincing and cinematically sophisticated. In the recovery of the mildly traumatic event (perhaps more in line with Freud's earlier ætiological theories from the *Studies on Hysteria* [Breuer and Freud 1893–1895] than with his then current preoccupations with the death drive, structural theory and signal anxiety), the protagonist's young girlfriend offers her doll to the cousin rather than to him, while his mother faces him with the unpalatable reality of the birth of a sibling. The seeds of our chemist's problems have been sown.

A little too simple? Of course it is! Not only that, but if we wanted to be pedantic we might also question why the analyst, in a patent breach of confidentiality, should telephone his jealous patient's wife to warn her that her husband is

Figure 1.1 Werner Krauss and Pavel Pavlov in *Secrets of a Soul* (Pabst 1926)

potentially dangerous, or maybe to ask her to keep away from him in order to facilitate the therapeutic process. Finally, when our protagonist repeats his potent attack with his knife turned towards, if not against, the analyst himself (both intercourse and murder, in a fusion of libidinal and aggressive drives), we may have wanted the therapist to interpret this behaviour as acting-out of the negative homosexual transference. Instead, the analysis ends here and a minute later so does also the film, with a delightfully fake tableau where our hero gives up his fishing hobby (illustrated in the musical accompaniment later added to the film by the melody of Schubert's *Die Forelle [The Trout]*) in order to become an enthusiastically good-enough father.

A little too quick? Of course it is! "Straightforward wish-fulfillment," comments Friedberg, is "a compensation for all that has been suffered in the course of the narrative" (Friedberg 1990, p. 51). Nor can one be too certain about the nature of the patient's pathology, a complex mixture of various phobic anxieties and counterphobic measures, obsessional jealousy, suppressed aggressivity, suicidal depression, sexual impotence and psychogenic infertility. But the expression of this very complexity, however condensed by the limitations of the medium – of *any* medium, we may add – far from being unconvincing, ultimately succeeds (*pace* Freud) in reflecting the complexity itself of the psychoanalytic perspective on the human condition.

*****

Alfred Hitchcock's *Spellbound*[10] is perhaps the most famous of all films about psychoanalysis. But is psychoanalysis what it is really about? In his wonderful fifty-hour-long interview to François Truffaut, from which I shall quote more than once, Hitchcock himself described his *Spellbound* as "just another manhunt story wrapped up in pseudo-psychoanalysis" (in Truffaut 1983, p. 165). I have good reasons to believe that I am not the only psychoanalyst to agree with such a view and we shall soon see why.

The film tells the story of John Ballantyne (Gregory Peck), a man pretending to be the new director of a mental institution, but soon exposed to be a former patient suffering from a phobia of black lines on white surfaces, amnesia, and a guilt complex. Unfairly accused of having murdered psychiatrist Dr Edwardes, Ballantyne believes himself to be responsible for it but only, as we'll later discover, because he displaces on this murder his guilt for having accidentally caused his brother's death when playing together as children. Psychoanalyst Dr Constance Petersen (Ingrid Bergman) promptly falls in love with him, is convinced of his innocence, and runs away with him to her own former training analyst (Michael Chekhov). To this analyst, Ballantyne will tell a revealing dream. As the truth about his childhood trauma and the real murderer of Dr Edwardes comes to the surface, analyst and patient will be free to live happily together ever after.

One psychoanalyst to be spellbound by *Spellbound* was Marshall Edelson. "At 17 I saw Ingrid Bergman and Michael Chekhov in Hitchcock's *Spellbound*," he wrote. "Under the spell of this movie I came to a sudden decision, which from then on I never questioned. I would have a psychoanalysis and then become a psychoanalyst. Later I was convinced – a slight European accent was enough – that my psychoanalyst looked and talked like Ingrid Bergman" (Edelson 1993).

As is well known, the detective story, or whodunnit à la Agatha Christie, was of little interest to Hitchcock because, he claimed, it "generates the kind of curiosity that is void of emotion . . . like a jigsaw or a crossword puzzle. No emotion. You simply wait to find out who committed the murder" (in Truffaut 1983, pp. 73–74). In the suspense thriller, on the other hand, the viewers are placed in a privileged position of knowledge because they know more than the detective: for instance, they have seen the villain lacing a drink with poison. This knowledge, however, as Cowie puts it, "is effectively 'useless' for though we know something may happen, we can neither act to prevent its occurrence, nor find out the answer sooner than the film narrates it to us. . . . [Thus the viewer] is made anxious on behalf of the protagonist" (Cowie 1997, p. 51). In the thriller, then, the audience, while being deprived of the element of *surprise*, is offered the gift of *suspense* which, according to Hitchcock, is "the most powerful means of holding onto the viewer's attention" (in Truffaut 1983, p. 72). *Spellbound* seems to be the exception to confirm the rule: because in fact it is precisely one of those whodunnit (or maybe a whodunnit-*not*) films which Hitchcock claims is of such little interest to him. Until near the end we, the viewers, do not know the truth about the fate of Dr Edwardes any better than the protagonists do.

Typical Hitchcock plots, or "basic formations" as Wood (1989, p. 241) calls them, involve guilty women (*Rebecca* 1940), psychopaths (*Psycho* 1960) and espionage or political intrigue (*Notorious* 1946). But the most common basic formation of all, also known as "the wrong man scenario," deals with the situation of an individual accused of a crime he has not committed: throughout Hitchcock's career a large number of his movies belong to that particular subgenre of thrillers.[11] Why was *Spellbound* such a prototype of anxiety-inducing situations for the Master of Suspense? Assuming we believe what he had to say about himself (and we know about his propensity to make things up), the answer may perhaps be found in an anecdote from his childhood he told Truffaut. "I must have been about four or five years old," Hitchcock recounts. "My father sent me to the police station with a note. The chief of police read it and locked me in a cell for five or ten minutes, saying, 'This is what we do to naughty boys.'" Asked why he was being punished, Hitchcock replied, "I haven't the faintest idea" (in Truffaut 1983, p. 24).

In this sense *Spellbound* is then a classical Hitchcock film. The original twist here is that, through the psychopathological devices of amnesia and of a guilt complex, the protagonist's main accuser is not some police chief or other such authority figure, but a part of his own mind, that is, his harsh superego, which has never forgiven him for the accidental death many years earlier of his brother. We can speculate that young John Ballantyne (does he not look about four or five years old, like young Alfred was when his father allegedly sent him to the police station?) might indeed have wished his sibling dead – not a rare occurrence even in the most loving of families – and therefore experienced the accident as the fulfillment of his murderous wishes. Hence the guilt complex that will be reactivated many years later on the ski slopes of Gabriel Valley.

Hitchcock cleverly manipulates his audience this way and that. At times the viewer identifies with Dr Constance Petersen in trusting that John Ballantyne must be the innocent victim of his own paranoid condition, if not also of some nasty conspiracy: when in doubt, look into his eyes. At other times, though, the viewer starts suspecting that he may not be so innocent after all: for instance, when we find old professor Alex Brulow lying in a dead-like position on the armchair after we have watched the Gregory Peck character going around the place with a razor in his hand, or when the police inspector stuns us with his announcement that a bullet was found in Dr Edwardes' body and that his death therefore was not accidental after all.

Ballantyne's self-accusation of this murder is echoed by another psychiatrist, Dr Murchison, identifying himself in his interpretation of the patient's dream as the Proprietor of the Gambling House (that is, as the Director of the Madhouse) and therefore as the real murderer. At times even psychopathic killers, we discover, are at the mercy of their own punishing superegos.

What about Ballantyne's famous dream, then? Before moving to it, let me say a few words about Salvador Dalí, who designed such a powerful visual representation of it, with all the sharpness required by Hitchcock in contrast with the more traditional handling of dream sequences through a blurred screen. (Compare this dream sequence, for instance, with the one in Pabst's *Secrets of a Soul* 1926.) André Breton in his *Manifeste du Surréalisme* had stated: "All credit must go to the discoveries of Freud. . . . A current of opinion is at last developing which will enable the explorer of the human mind to extend his investigations much further" (Breton 1924). In the introductory essay of the catalogue to the Tate Gallery 1980 exhibition of Dalí's paintings, Simon Wilson wrote: "Any critical account of the art of Salvador Dalí or of Surrealism in general must take as its point of departure Sigmund Freud whose influence . . . was absolutely fundamental" (Wilson 1980, p. 9). Freud, of course, a son of the Enlightenment, had no patience for any sort of surrealistic irrationalism.[12]

Let us also remember that Dalí was influenced by Max Ernst, the artist who had pioneered an approach based on the visual quality of dreams. He was followed by René Magritte and by Giorgio de Chirico's dreamlike metaphysical paintings. With this background and with his experience of working for the cinema with Buñuel some twenty years earlier, it is not surprising that Dalí, who happened to be in the United States at the time, should have accepted producer David O. Selznick's invitation to design the set for the dream sequence in *Spellbound*. Hitchcock recalls: "Dalí had some strange ideas; he wanted a statue to crack like a shell falling apart, with ants crawling all over it, and underneath, there would be Ingrid Bergman, covered by the ants! It just wasn't possible" (in Truffaut 1983, p. 165).

Because the interpretation of the dream is used in *Spellbound* as a way of unlocking a mystery through the recovery of a memory that will open the Royal Road to the final dramatic unfolding of the narrative, the attribute of "pseudo-psychoanalysis" is appropriate. The function of dreams, at least in classical psychoanalysis, is quite different: to express in a distorted form not a suppressed memory but an unconscious repressed wish. Here we have instead a sort of symbolic decoding of the various elements of the manifest dream content, based on the clever speculations of two doctors (antagonistic to each other in the story, but allied in this hermeneutic endeavour) rather than on the patient's own free associations. The tall chimney therefore must be a tree, the man with the beard a psychoanalyst, and the wheel a revolver. Such conjectures are as cute as they are implausible, and anyway have little to do with psychoanalysis. But then Hitchcock himself will tell you that he does not give a toss about plausibility; though again, one should not take him too literally.

Ballantyne's dream gives me the opportunity for a brief digression away from *Spellbound*. I wish to consider how even films which do not contain oneiric scenes may nevertheless resonate in the viewers almost as if the films themselves were dreams. By adopting a language of images edited in a free-associative style, or by means of special camera movements, lighting, filters, soundtrack and various other technical devices, such movies can create a deliberately surreal atmosphere that conveys a dreamlike impression to the viewers. A contemporary master of this art is the Czech filmmaker Jan Svankmajer who, with the help of sophisticated animation, offers his audiences images and stories finely suspended between the magical and the disturbingly uncanny – just like dreams.[13]

We may further suggest here that the association between dreams and movies, *any* movies almost regardless of their form or content, is profoundly instilled in our culture. I still remember that, as children growing up in the 1950s, when reporting our dreams we always mentioned whether they were in colour or black-and-white. I suppose that children of the previous generation may have commented on their dreams as being silent or talkies, while contemporary kids may question whether or not they see their dreams in 3D. Films are not dreams, of course, but they share with them a number of important features. To begin with, they have in common the purpose, among others, to express latent unconscious wishes through their manifest contents, and both utilize, for the purpose of circumventing repression, similar mechanisms. These include (in films, especially through editing) condensation, displacement, symbolic expression, secondary revision and distortions of time and space. While Freud, as we have pointed out, was indifferent or even sceptical about cinema, his colleague Otto Rank had noticed that "cinematography . . . in numerous ways reminds us of the dream-work" (Rank 1914 p. 4).

Eberwein (1984) suggests a similarity between the film screen and the dream screen as places of both fusion and separation. The concept of a dream screen, which Winnicott described as "a place into or onto which a dream might be dreamed" (Winnicott 1968, p. 303) was originally developed by Bertram D. Lewin: "I conceived the idea that dreams contained a special structure which I named the *dream screen*. . . . I thought of the dream as a picture or a projected set of images, and for the reception of these images I predicated a screen, much like the one we see in the artificial night of a dark motion-picture house before the drama has radiated forth from the window of the projection box" (Lewin 1953, p. 174). It may not be a coincidence that Hollywood has always been described as a *Traumfabrik*, a "dream factory" (Ehrenburg 1931). And, I shall add, a factory of a few nightmares too.

Let us now return to *Spellbound*. As well as questioning how Ballantyne's dream was interpreted in the movie, we also have to contend with the important issues of transference and countertransference, hinted at in the film but never properly addressed – another and more serious instance of pseudo-psychoanalysis.[14] Not only does Dr Petersen predict that her lover/patient will soon develop a negative transference towards her (which she will bear with professional stoicism), but also she experiences her own erotic countertransference-at-first-sight towards him, which she acts out. These events combine to constitute a core theme in the movie. "I am here as your doctor only," she whispers, passionately kissing her patient. "It's nothing to do with love. Nothing at all." The best line in the whole film.

By the way, as Andrew Britton (1985) points out, while the film's text accounts for Ballantyne's neurotic problems as being the reactivation of repressed memories, its subtext suggests that his anxiety is also aroused by the threat of his analyst's active female sexuality. Apparently, during the filming Ingrid Bergman went to Hitchcock as she had problems with some of her lines. She was clearly upset, but he reassured her: "Ingrid," he said, "it's only a movie!" Yet, movies

Figure 1.2 Ingrid Bergman, Gregory Peck and Michael Chekhov in *Spellbound* (Hitchcock 1945)

were his life. "What is drama, after all," he told Truffaut, "but life with the dull bits cut out" (in Truffaut 1983, p. 103).

*****

Directed by anthropologist and filmmaker Hugh Brody, *Nineteen Nineteen*[15] is a British production which occupies a special place in the small but important subgenre of films on psychoanalysis. When it was released in Britain in 1985, soon after its premiere at the Berlin Film Festival, the critic Philip French, comparing it to Pabst's *Secrets of a Soul*, Huston's *Freud: The Secret Passion* and Hitchcock's *Spellbound*, wrote in his review on *The Observer*: "with *Nineteen Nineteen* the cinema has at last reached some maturity in its approach to Freud, psychoanalysis and their place in history" (French 1985).[16]

The film recounts a day-long meeting in 1970 of two former patients of Freud's: émigré Russian aristocrat Alexander Sherbàtof (Paul Scofield) still living in Vienna, and Sophie Rubin (Maria Schell) visiting him from New York where she had emigrated many years earlier. Now in their late sixties, they reminisce about their personal histories, their emotional problems, and their analytic relationship with Freud in 1919, on the background of the large-scale social events that were shaking Europe.

Nineteen Nineteen has a complex structure which consists of four interrelated levels of discourse through which the narrative unfolds, flowing seamlessly across from one to the other.

The location is Vienna, mostly in Alexander's sombre "dungeon" or "lair" as he calls it, in various exteriors and, towards the end, in Freud's house, now a museum, in 19 Berggaße. The film title, as well as the year when its protagonists were in analysis with Freud, may also be a reference to this address, twice repeated "19–19." That building was an important point of reference in their existences. We the viewers are given access, and it feels almost a privilege, to the interactions and dialogues taking place between Alexander and Sophie concerning themselves as they are now, in their late sixties, and the relationship, suspended between hostility and cautious affection, developing between them. We see them traveling in trams, making tea, smoking cigarettes, placing a bunch of anemones in a vase, sitting on a bench in the park, drawing curtains. . . . Also, in the present time, we are spectators to their recalling of events, impressions and fantasies related to their personal and collective history.

In flashback we are offered the reliving of the past, either in colour during Alexander's and Sophie's troubled adolescence, on and off the couch, or in archival black-and-white still photographs and newsreels. On the background of the large historical stage of the Bolshevik Revolution, the First World War, the rise of Fascism and the *Anschluß* of Austria – events which, like psychoanalysis itself, have shaped the past century – *Nineteen Nineteen* "dares to wonder how we locate personal history within the social memory of the wider world" (Sekoff 1996, p. 48).

And finally, again in flashback, we enter the *sancta sanctorum* of Freud's consulting room, where an adolescent Alexander (now played by Colin Firth in one of his first roles) and an equally young Sophie (Claire Higgins) lie on the famous couch to discuss their "material." Both we, the viewers, and they, the analysands, (wearing Loden coats, woolly jumpers and leather gloves to protect themselves from the postwar winter cold) never actually see Freud, but only hear him speak from the analyst's chair through Frank Finlay's reassuring, disembodied, off-screen voice.

This device of not showing the analyst means that "although he is omnipresent in the emotional memories of his analysands, [he] has managed to render perceptible that 'absent third party' that is indispensable for the economics and the dynamics of any psychoanalytic session," while the intermingling of different temporalities "almost manages to give a cinematographic representation of that very important Freudian notion of *Nachträglichkeit*" (de Mijolla 1994, pp. 197–198).

The protagonists' biographies are based on two of Freud's celebrated case studies published around the year 1919. Alexander shares many traits with the so-called Wolf Man (1918) while the Sophie character is clearly based on the case of the homosexual girl whom Freud wrote about in 1920. Problems of gender and sexual identity are central to the pathology of the former and to the personality of the latter. The Wolf Man's condition was understood by Freud as deriving from an earlier infantile neurosis. The detailed analysis of his vivid childhood dream helped to unearth early fantasies and memories, both exciting and frightening (in particular a Primal Scene about his parents during sexual intercourse) which formed the basis of his later psychopathology: intense anxiety, phobias and a variety of obsessional symptoms. "The result of the dream," Freud concluded, "was not so much the triumph of a masculine current, as a reaction against a feminine and passive one" (Freud 1918, p. 112). This would account for this patient's confused gender identifications and later peculiar taste in sexual object-choice, as portrayed in the film by Alexander's "two kinds of women": idealized angels like his sister and the exciting whores he describes as "shit."

Sophie, on the other hand, bears similarities with that "beautiful and clever girl of eighteen [who] had aroused displeasure and concern in her parents by the devoted adoration with which she pursued a certain 'society lady'" (Freud 1920b, p. 147). When her mother gives birth to a baby, the patient (now a 16-year-old) experiences a violent reoccurrence of Oedipal fantasies. As a result she feels betrayed by her father and ends up repudiating "her wish for a child, her love of men, and the feminine role in general. . . . What actually happened," Freud tells us, "was the most extreme case. She changed into a man and took her mother in place of her father as the object of her love" (Freud 1920b, p. 158). Having emphatically stated that he did not consider her in any way neurotic, Freud understands her homosexuality as stemming from her unconscious wish and rivalrous envy for her own mother, for whom the society lady is clearly a substitute.

In Brody's film Sophie comes to Vienna to reminisce and remember. Alexander instead is already there, living quite literally inside a museum of memorabilia. As in psychoanalysis, memory is not merely about the recovery of our past but about providing a deeper meaning to our present. "As makers of transference," writes Sekoff, "we are not only captives of the past, but captors – capturing others within our repetitive patterns" (Sekoff 1996, p. 47). However hard they try, though, they cannot get rid of their existential burden any more than Lady Macbeth could wash the blood off her hands. In spite of their analyses with a man, Freud, from whom, in Alexander's own words, "Nothing escaped . . . nothing," each of them has failed in his or her peculiar way to come to terms with, and integrate, their past lives into the present ones.

The emphasis in *Nineteen Nineteen*, and here we can identify a major difference with other movies dealing directly with the psychoanalytic profession, is not on psychoanalysis as a means for discovering some hidden secret from our childhood. Unlike in those films there are no symbolic doors and keys unlocking repressed truths. There are no technically or artistically sophisticated oneiric sequences to be decoded. There are no Freudian grand hermeneutic gestures of interpretation as insightful turning points in the protagonists' life vicissitudes. In fact *Nineteen Nineteen*, while giving an authentic sense of what the psychoanalytic experience is about (or at least was then, in 1919), remains ambivalent, and perhaps healthily so, about its therapeutic value.

There is a dramatic moment in the film when Alexander confesses he can remember only what he withheld from Freud: "Only the things I never told him. He took everything else." Here Freud is portrayed as a thief of memories, and Alexander as the victim of an emotional robbery who needs to protect himself by locking his mind away, though his memories will go on festering. Both Alexander and Sophie might have gained profound insights from their sessions on the couch back in 1919, but both of them have also remained psychologically damaged individuals, affected perhaps by that incurably normal human misery which Freud himself had predicted we are all doomed to suffer. Does Brody's movie ultimately blame Freud and analysis – or the patients, or history, or life itself – for their failures?

Psychoanalysis has moved on, in the cinema as it has in its practice, from a concern with reconstructions based on Freud's own metaphor of our profession as "archaeology of the mind" (Freud 1937b) to one about the profound interpersonal conscious and unconscious meanings of relationships and interpersonal communication, of transference and countertransference. The analyst is "a new object" (Loewald 1960), as well as a transferential one. The present becomes a narrative in its own right even if imbued, as it always is, with all the layers of significance accumulated from past experiences. Furthermore, we are all implicated: observers affect what is being observed, the readers are in the text, the therapist's feelings are part of the analytic process, the public belongs to the show; which takes us back, by the way, to *Nineteen Nineteen*'s historical dimension of private worlds.

While Alexander and Sophie "ostensibly have nothing in common except their analyst, they are such opposites that their pairing is brilliant," comments Hoffman (1986, p. 70). In the few hours they spend together in Vienna for what is likely to remain the most truly therapeutic encounter in their lives, they "vividly, painfully, mournfully reach back to the past – not only to solve a puzzle or to paste together a story – but to touch once more the fire, the aliveness of their passions" (Sekoff 1996, p. 47).

Figure 1.3 Maria Schell and Paul Scofield in *Nineteen Nineteen* (Brody 1985)

The climax of *Nineteen Nineteen* then is not the discovery of deep-seated causes of current psychopathology but the moment when Alexander, with a desperately naive gesture, asks Sophie to remain in Vienna with him, her predictable reply (she knows only too well about repetition compulsion), and the intimate embrace they exchange when a taxi is already there to take her back.

*****

The inclusion of the film *Il Postino*[17] in this chapter on our "young profession" requires some justification. As many readers will know, that movie is actually *not* about a psychoanalyst, nor about an analysand. However, as you will find out in the next few pages, I am going to argue that the close relationship that gradually develops between Mario the postman (Massimo Troisi) and Neruda the poet (Philippe Noiret), a relationship which is at the very core of the film's narrative, shares many features with what normally takes place in our own analytic consulting rooms.

WANTED: POSTMAN WITH BICYCLE, reads the notice outside the village post office.

Only a temporary job, but almost tailor-made for Mario, an introverted and uneducated yet sharply insightful young man, protagonist of Michael Radford's delightfully bittersweet, humane, humourous, moving yet never sentimental (and, incidentally, enormously successful) comedy *Il Postino*.[18] The job involves carrying the mail to just one illustrious addressee, the Chilean poet Pablo Neruda, who was exiled in the early 1950s to a Southern Italian island (the film was shot in

Salina and Procida) because of his Communist views. Every day Mario pedals up to the poet's new residence, a villa located on the top of a hill surrounded by wild Mediterranean vegetation and overlooking the sea. Mario is carrying a leather bag full of correspondence: mostly, at least in his adolescent mind fueled by newsreel mythology, love letters from adoring women all over the world.

At first, of course, Mario and Neruda hardly talk. What is there to be said, anyway, between them? Intrigued by his own thoughts and feelings, the postman cannot find the words to express them and the poet has better things to do than listen to him. But, as the relationship develops, Mario finds an interlocutor and, with it, a voice: tentative at first, when he dares, after a farcical rehearsal in front of the mirror, to ask the poet for an autograph in the hope that this will impress his girlfriends in Naples – then progressively more secure. In Neruda-the-Man he gradually discovers the parental figure to identify with and idealize; in Neruda-the-Poet the language to make sense of his own inner world. If Mario's real father is a silent, down-to-earth (or down-to-sea) fisherman with little understanding of his son's existential problems ("I am tired of being a man," Mario says echoing Neruda's words), his dead mother is entirely absent. However, the mother is present in the guises of nature, both literally in the external world and literarily in Neruda's, and then Mario's own, poetry: an all-embracing, all-containing and nurturing sea surrounding the beautiful, part lush, part desert island.

The film has the structure, familiar to fiction readers and cinemagoers alike, of a *Bildungsroman*. Witnessed by the poet himself, Mario's development into a mature man culminates in his achievement of potency which finds its expression at three different but interconnected levels. The first level is *sexual* through his relationship, as passionate as it is clumsy, to maidenly sensuous waitress Beatrice, whom he eventually marries with Neruda's help and blessing. The second level is *literary* as Mario starts reading and producing verse himself, and even suggesting to his own Master an excellent adjective ("sad") to describe what fishing-nets look like. It is not a coincidence that he will unselfconsciously create his first metaphor when listening to Neruda's lyrical description of the sea: "I feel . . . weird and seasick," he says, "like a boat tossing around . . . words." Finally, his third level of maturing is *political* and is achieved by tentatively opposing a local Mafioso boss and through an ill-fated involvement with a Communist demonstration, where he is invited to read one of his own Neruda-inspired poems to the crowd.

Part of the fascination of *Il Postino* consists in creatively immersing a real and contemporary character, the poet Pablo Neruda (here portrayed with biographical accuracy), in an entirely fictional situation. But if the filmmaker's fantasy interplays with history, the external world also intrudes, and most tragically, into the artistic work. As soon as the shooting of *Il Postino* was over Massimo Troisi, the actor in the title role, prematurely died. In the film, Mario is killed at a mass rally during an incident with the police: a conclusion ideologically and aesthetically unnecessary perhaps, but also providing the viewers who are aware of Troisi's premature death with a powerfully uncanny experience of life imitating art.

I would like to suggest here that Neruda is also Mario's "psychoanalyst" The "sessions" are represented by the postman's uphill journeys by bicycle, at regular intervals, to the poet's villa. Such ritualized visits, charged as they are for Mario with meaningful words and silences, part monologues and part dialogues, readily become opportunities for him to learn about love, literature, relationships, and ultimately himself. A central mechanism in this therapeutic process is identification: "I'd like to be a poet too," says Mario, and asks Neruda how to become one – a wish that the latter only superficially discourages ("You'll get as fat as me!"). The postman/patient identifies with the poet/analyst: his wish to become like him is so frequent in clinical practice that it could be hyperbolically argued that, in fantasy at least, all analyses are training analyses!

Mario's journeys to the poet's villa, at the same time, are also more regressive explorations of Primal Scene unconscious fantasies, as exemplified by the love letters he delivers and is explicitly curious about to Neruda, as well as by the poet's sensual relationship with his wife Matilde. The first time Mario finds them hugging, he modestly hides away. Later, however, after he has himself established a sexual relationship with Beatrice, he allows himself some vicarious pleasure by watching the Nerudas dance a passionate tango.

We can recognize a number of important elements, crucial to the film's narrative and characterizations, which are also integral aspects of the psychoanalytic experience. For example, our postman alternates between blaming Neruda for his love problems with Beatrice and expecting him to resolve them (a situation not unfamiliar to psychoanalysts). The name Beatrice is itself evocative, being also the name of the woman who inspired Dante Alighieri, whose presence in the background as the Father of all Poets reminds one of the part played in many analyses by Sigmund Freud, the Father of all

Figure 1.4 Philippe Noiret and Massimo Troisi in *Il Postino* (Radford 1994)

Psychoanalysts. (Neruda and Freud, by the way, were both candidates, though only the former successfully, for the Nobel Prize; and *Il Postino* for five Academy awards.)

Neruda tells Mario that "poetry is the experience of feeling," a statement that could as well apply to psychoanalysis: they both provide alternative perspectives on the world, and a language to describe it. It is significant, I think, that our hero is a postman, he who "carries across" (*trans-fers*, in Latin) emotionally loaded messages; and that his conversations with the poet often revolve around the subject of metaphors, a word which in the film becomes itself a metaphor for all that is not prosaic in life. It is after all primarily through their interpretative work, which depends on such rhetorical devices as metaphors and analogies, that analysts help analysands understand the complex connections between different sets of thoughts, emotions and relationships. Furthermore, having the same etymology as transference, the concept of metaphor seems ideal to indicate the associations between literature and psychoanalysis and, in its audio and visual representations, cinema itself. Words, the stuff both poetry and the talking cure are made of, are powerful. Even Beatrice's bigoted, but not idiotic, aunt Rosa, constantly worried about her niece's virginity, can state that "a man is not far off with his hands when he starts touching you with his words!"

Neruda's countertransferential relationship to Mario (as the *postino* has always suspected, but also denied until its reality becomes overwhelmingly painful) is coloured by ambivalence, and not just or even primarily because of its homosexual undertones. The poet, at least in Mario's projective fantasies, is partly the benevolent parental figure we assume he has never had, partly the detached, indifferent, cold professional – almost a caricature of a psychoanalyst – ready to forget him as soon as their "contract" is over, as soon as he can return to Chile and there is no more correspondence to be delivered. When Neruda embraces Mario before leaving the island, the termination of their relationship is as deeply felt by both of them as the one at the end of a good analysis. "You left something behind for me," says Mario, who is now ready to internalize the poet/father/analyst and get on with life on his own, though not without much sadness. But then his mentor fails to keep in touch: when at long last, after more than one year, Mario receives a letter from Chile, and it is a disappointingly impersonal message from the poet's secretary asking for the return of some effects left behind in the by-now-dilapidated villa. Mario feels devastated but still tries to rationalize Neruda's behaviour: "Why should he remember me? . . . I think it's quite normal," he says. But there are bitter tears in his eyes.

Radford's *Il Postino* may not be what is conventionally understood as a psychoanalytic film – assuming such an object exists at all. Attempting to interpret the unconscious meanings of an exiled Communist poet's behaviour and verse, or of an islander's everyday life preoccupations, would have been a futile exercise. The film has minimal symbolism in its imagery, no dream sequences, no scenes taking place in a mental institution or in a therapist's consulting room, no display of violence, perversion or psychopathology. And yet the description of a process of maturation through an intense and regular personal rapport full of transferential and countertransferential connotations, which is central to this movie, has much in common in its structure and functions with the psychoanalytic relationship. In this respect, viewing *Il Postino* through a psychoanalytic lens by drawing parallels between the two situations can hopefully enrich and deepen our understanding of both.

Notes

1. Another analyst made popular by television in the last few years is Dr Jennifer Melfi (played by Lorraine Bracco), the attractive therapist of mobster Tony Soprano (the late James Gandolfini) in the groundbreaking and hugely successful drama series *The Sopranos* (Chase 1999–2007).
2. See, for instance, the title of the important book on American cinema *Psychiatry and the Cinema*. In their "Preface to the Second Edition," authors Glen Gabbard and Krin Gabbard wrote: "Since the appearance of our first edition in 1987, psychiatry has continued to distance itself from psychoanalysis and psychotherapy. Nevertheless, in the cinematic world, the emphasis remains on the talking cure. . . . Hence, we continue to use the term *psychiatry* in the broadest possible sense to encompass all mental health professionals, especially those who practice psychotherapy" (Gabbard and Gabbard 1999, pp. xix–xx).
3. *Secrets of a Soul [Geheimnisse einer Seele]* (Germany 1926). Directed by Georg Wilhelm Pabst. Written by Karl Abraham, Hans Neumann et al. Starring Werner Krauss (Martin Fellman), Ruth Weyher (his wife), and Pavel Pavlov (Dr Orth).
4. The English-language literature on this film includes Chodorkoff and Baxter (1974), Browne and McPherson (1980), Friedberg (1990), MacDonald (1990), Ries (1995), Sklarew (1999), Marcus (2001), Brandell (2004) and Gifford (2004).
5. Consistent with his views, only a few months earlier Freud had declined to meet Samuel Goldwyn and to accept his substantial offer of $100,000 to cooperate with him on a film on love.
6. This case was based on one of Abraham's patients.
7. It would be incorrect to assume such analysts to be mostly male and their patients female. In a survey of the topic Gabbard and Gabbard (1989) have found only nine movies where a male therapist falls for a female patient, compared with at least nineteen where it is a female therapist to be swept away by countertransference love for a male patient. At the same time, these authors have found only two films where a female therapist effectively treats a male patient, with thirty-three films where the situation is reversed.
8. In 1953 Pabst made a film in Rome's studios of Cinecittà, *Cose da pazzi*, now presumed lost. The film concerns a woman committed by mistake to a mental institution, from which she is eventually rescued by an enlightened doctor.
9. The powerful realization of these dream sequences reminds us of the notorious ones by Salvador Dalí, not only for Buñuel, but also, twenty years later, for Alfred Hitchcock's "psychoanalytic" *Spellbound* (1945, see below).
10. *Spellbound* (United States 1945). Directed by Alfred Hitchcock. Written by Ben Hecht et al., from Frances Beeding's novel *The House of Dr Edwardes*. Starring Ingrid Bergman (Dr Constance Petersen), Gregory Peck (John Ballantyne), and Michael Chekhov (Dr Alexander Brulov).
11. See *The Lodger* (1927), *The 39 Steps* (1935), *Suspicion* (1941), *Saboteur* (1942), *Strangers on a Train* (1951), *To Catch a Thief* (1955), *The Wrong Man* (1956), *North by Northwest* (1959) and *Frenzy* (1972).

12. The meeting that actually took place in Freud's house in London in 1938 between him and Dalí was farcically portrayed in *Hysteria,* a play by Terry Johnson (1993) first performed at the Royal Court Theatre in London that year.
13. A good example is his recent feature *Surviving Life* (Svankmajer 2010) which happens to deal explicitly with this most psychoanalytic of material.
14. We must wonder what Dr May Romm, Hitchcock's psychiatric adviser, had to say about this and other aspects of the film. Romm happened to be the psychoanalyst of *Spellbound*'s own producer, David O. Selznick, and she was to become the Hollywood analyst *par excellence.*
15. *Nineteen Nineteen* (Great Britain 1985). Directed by Hugh Brody. Written by Hugh Brody and Michael Ignatieff. Starring Paul Scofield (Alexander Sherbàtof), Maria Schell (Sophie Rubin), Colin Firth (Alexander Sherbàtof as a young man), Clare Higgins (Sophie Rubin as a young woman), and Diana Quick (Anna).
16. Readers interested in this film are referred to Berger (1985) and Brody and Brearley (2003).
17. *Il Postino* (Italy 1994). Directed by Michael Radford. Written by Furio Scarpelli et al., from Antonio Skármeta's novel *Ardente Paciencia.* Starring Massimo Troisi (Mario), Philippe Noiret (Pablo Neruda), and Maria Grazia Cucinotta (Beatrice).
18. *Il Postino* was for several years the largest grossing non-English-language film ever made.

Chapter 2

...and the oldest one
Films on prostitution

From Chapter One where we discussed films on our relatively new profession of psychoanalysis we now make the rather risqué leap to examining some movies depicting a profession which, for reasons not altogether obvious, has the reputation of being not only disreputable but also the oldest of them all. Feature films about prostitution are plenty and have approached their subject from a variety of perspectives within different cinematic genres, ranging from the dramatic to the comical and the pornographic, and covering a wide number of themes. Some of the best-known movies on prostitutes, besides those discussed here, are *Pandora's Box* (Pabst 1929), *Breakfast at Tiffany's* (Edwards 1961), *Klute* (Pakula 1971), *Jeanne Dielman* (Akermann 1975) *Mona Lisa* (Jordan 1986), *Pretty Woman* (Marshall 1990) and *Leaving Las Vegas* (Figgis 1995).

I am well aware of the social complexities surrounding the practice of selling and buying sexual favours for money, and of the dangers of falling into the trap of moralizing prostitutes and their clients or of pathologizing them. It is a trap not always avoided by either filmmakers making movies about them or psychoanalysts having them in therapy. While prostitution could be seen as consisting of a straightforward transaction between consenting partners about physical interactions regulated by a financial contract, there is in fact much more involved in the practice of this oldest of professions. One of the main issues to be considered concerns the exercise of power: it is mostly the client who, having paid the money, has all the control, possession and authority over the prostitute (he who pays the piper calls the tune), though at times roles within these most impermanent of relationships can also get reversed. Who is using whom? Are punters exploiting whores or is it the other way round? The only thing we can be certain about is that pimps exploit them both: that is the very essence of their job.[1]

Most women and men who get involved, often at a young age, in the sex trade are forced into it by unfortunate or even tragic circumstances: because of unworked-through experiences of deprivation or abuse in their childhood, because of current unbearable financial need (for instance in order to support a drug addiction) combined with a real or perceived lack of other options, because of their emotional dependence on individuals taking advantage of them, or because of a combination of some or all of the above factors.

However, an awareness of these reasons should not prevent us from recognizing the psychological motives leading a young person to choose to become a prostitute. These may include a low self-esteem; the conflictual wish to indulge in otherwise unacceptable perverse activities; a difficulty in assessing whom to trust, often making them mistrust those who could really help them, or blindly believe good of those who only intend to hurt and take advantage of them; the hope that their career in the sex trade may give them access to an otherwise unreachable exciting and glamorous life, or at least to the consumer goods that allegedly represent it; and, perhaps most importantly, the forbidden fantasy that it would allow them to find the true love they so desperately need.

Whatever overdetermined combination of reasons that might lead a person to work as a prostitute, we cannot ignore the emotional suffering so often associated with their lives. If we begin to examine some of the psychological aspects, many of them unconscious, that characterize how prostitutes experience themselves, we will find, for instance, that many of them have an ambivalent relationship to their own bodies, oscillating between idealization and denigration, between an overvaluation of their physical qualities and utter disgust for them. They can end up treating their bodies as if they only consisted of part objects, with a potential for being financially rewarding but also disconnected from the rest of their selves. A relevant issue here concerns the psychological mechanism of splitting: an indispensable defense for prostitutes (and possibly for their clients too), whereby the sexual activities taking place in the course of their encounters are kept separate from the sexual activities they may engage in with other partners, and indeed from the interpersonal relationships they may entertain with anyone else, such as family and friends. More specifically, in order to survive psychologically from their activities, prostitutes need to put all sensations and feelings they may have for their clients in brackets. Any emotional involvement with clients would lead to inevitable disappointment and suffering; something which, in many movies and in real life as well, prostitutes may only learn when it is too late.

Of course, not all whores are female. A classic film about a male prostitute is John Schlesinger's *Midnight Cowboy* (1969): we watch Joe (John Voight) travel by coach to New York City from Texas, full of rather unrealistic hopes to make an easy buck (this word also happens to be his surname) by selling his sexual favours for cash – ideally to attractive wealthy women but also (why not?) to anyone else willing to pay. Brief flashbacks provide the viewers with an insight into the sexual abuse and background of neglect Joe had suffered as a child in the absence of a male figure with whom to identify.

From its title, *Midnight Cowboy*,[2] one would expect a Western, but this film is instead what I would dare to call an *Eastern*. A gum-chewing cowboy, attached to a transitional transistor radio like a Winnicottian toddler to his teddy-bear, travels Eastway to the Big Apple. His grand plan is to conquer that city by exploiting its allegedly countless sex-starved "rich bitches" (his words, not mine) or, failing to score with them, the "faggots of 42nd Street" (again, his words): "Begging for it," he confidently asserts, "paying for it." His various sexual encounters, however, end in predictable failures, either of the violent or the farcical kind. This cowboy's cows, for instance, do not let themselves be meekly rounded up by him, quite the opposite, and instead of paying for his potent services they expect him to pay them! The turning point for Joe is a chance meeting with Rico (Dustin Hoffman), a vulnerable and cynical, limping dropout, barely surviving in the cold world of the metropolis through petty crime, cunning and a sense of humour. Their relationship, mutually exploitative at first, will develop into a true friendship that will profoundly change the lives of them both.[3] Having built their lives around the illusion of repairing the damage they have suffered through the exploitation of others (including each other), they will eventually realize in a final few days of true caring for one another that friendship is possible after all.

It may be appropriate in this context for us to consider the common fantasy that there is a close association between prostitution and psychoanalysis. If psycho-analysis, as Freud stated in his letter to Jung of 6 December 1906, "is in essence a cure through love" (quoted by Jones 1955, p. 485) and we get paid to offer it, then our new profession is not that different from the oldest one. We may not like it much, but we psychoanalysts, not unlike prostitutes, also sell our time and love for money – and analysands are not infrequently keen to remind us of it, as if our hard work had no other motivation than a financial one. This is not the place to discuss the complex issue of the function of money in psychoanalysis; it may however be relevant to report here that many years ago I was amused to find out the contrasting attitudes of two of my patients about money. One insisted on paying me cash because, she said, "I could never give you a cheque! Cheques are too personal, having my own handwriting and even my name printed on them." The other always paid his bills with cheques because, he said, "I could never give you cash! Cash is dirty, cash is what you pay whores with."[4]

We should add that many individuals visiting prostitutes are not just, or even not primarily, in search of a sexual experience, but rather of some company, of a chance to be listened to and understood (others may apply for psychotherapy instead). At least some of these punters may be secretly hoping that, in the process, they will meet one of those mythical tarts with a heart – a character-type frequently met in films on prostitution – who would cure them of their loneliness and despair. I remember an impressive play on this theme by the Italian writer Dacia Maraini, *Only Prostitutes Marry in May* (1973), consisting of a long, emotionally charged dialogue, or session, between a prostitute and her distressed client. The complementary fantasy here concerns those punters who get involved with prostitutes for the grandiose and mostly doomed-to-failure wish to rescue them from their condition.

On all of these and other relevant issues, films on prostitution such as those discussed in the chapter, as well as the material produced by prostitutes in analysis, may provide new insights.

*****

Cabiria and Lilya are two young prostitutes. Their stories, half a century apart, take place in different parts of Europe, and in different films. Cabiria is the working-class girl portrayed in Federico Fellini's early masterpiece. We watch her walking the streets of Rome in search of punters, dreaming of finding her great love, laughing and crying with the same spontaneity, and somehow just about managing to remain free to the very last frame of the film. Lilya is the adolescent from the former Soviet Union in a disturbing movie by Lukas Moodysson. She moves to Sweden to run away from her miserable conditions back at home, only to become the victim of heartless sex traffickers removing her passport and with it her sense of identity, forcing her into prostitution, despair and, ultimately, suicide.

Cabiria and Lylia. Both young, unhappy girls. Both victims of cruel circumstances. Yet, how different their stories! Of Cabiria's childhood and family life we are told nothing in the film, while in the case of Lilya we are shown the extent of the physical and psychological neglect and the cruel abandonment she had to endure, setting her up for the rest of her brief existence. While Cabiria is a survivor, Lilya seems to have no chance at all. While the resources of the Roman young girl may allow her to eventually find a way out of her sorry condition, Lilya's personality, battered by the extremes of the abuse, betrayal and exploitation forced upon her by her family first and by callous pimps next, can only lead her to a tragic end.

The eponymous protagonist of Federico Fellini's film *Cabiria*[5] is played by his own wife Giulietta Masina. Cabiria is at the same time a clown and a streetwise streetwalker, a vulnerable Chaplinesque waif and a resilient woman, a lost soul and an angry fighter. She goes through her miserable existence hoping that some miracle – from either a chance encounter with Mister Right or from the equally improbable intervention of the *Madonna del Divino Amore* – may allow her to change her life for good. Instead, everything seems to conspire against her and even what appears to give her some hope of repairing her damaged existence

Figure 2.1 Giulietta Masina in *Cabiria* (Fellini 1956)

Figure 2.2 Oksana Akinshina in *Lilya-4-Ever* (Moodysson 2002)

bitterly disappoints her. This is repeated again and again, as if she lacked a basic capacity to learn from past experiences. Yet, there is something wonderfully uplifting about her personality as, between a smile and a tear, she is always ready to recover from the upsets she encounters at every step of her existence, and be reborn like a Phoenix from the fire of her unhappiness.

Cabiria's sad vicissitudes take place in Rome (or rather its outskirts), a city still physically and morally gutted by the scars of war, which contrasts but also complements the glitzy and decadent one Fellini will show us four years later in *La Dolce Vita* (1960), and already hinted at in the episode with *divo* playboy Amedeo Nazzari. She is accompanied throughout her journey by the music of Nino Rota, Fellini's regular composer, whose tunes are taken up in turn by various minor characters in the background: "turned into a mambo by street musicians, then passed on to a band in a nightclub, given to an accordion in a field and to a solo piano at a music hall, and [in the celebrated final sequence] taken up by a strolling company of high-spirited teenagers" (Graham 1998). It is worth remembering here that Fellini played music on his sets during almost every scene, which was possible because, like many Italian directors of his generation, he did not record the dialogue when shooting but dubbed the words in at a later time.

Here I would like to focus on the converse of the common rescue fantasy[6]: the fantasy of *being rescued* which I think pervades Fellini's film throughout. Indeed, the story begins with the dramatic instance of Cabiria being saved from drowning after a sexual encounter (and showing little gratitude to the local people who had rescued her). As we shall see in more detail in our discussion of *Amores Perros* in Chapter Five, both sets of fantasies (rescuing others or being rescued by them) are represented in the Greek myth of Orpheus and Eurydice. Like Eurydice, Cabiria keeps hoping that some Orpheus in the shape of a successful actor, a phoney hypnotizer, a gentle accountant with the remarkable name of Oscar, if not the

Holy Virgin herself, may rescue her from the hell of a life on the streets: from her murderous pimp, abusive punters, vulgar colleagues, and the incursions by overzealous police officers. But although no one is ultimately likely to offer her what she needs, Cabiria never resigns herself to her misfortunes and never gives up believing that she will, eventually, find some happiness.

A psychologically significant theme emerging from the narrative of Moodysson's *Lilya-4-Ever*[7] concerns the issue of putting one's trust in others, especially in those (such as parents, other older relatives, and teachers) who should be responsible for the care of younger generations.

In his classic book *Childhood and Society* (1960), Erik Erikson points out that the tension between trust and mistrust is of central importance in the first eighteen months of psychological development for the establishment of a child's future confidence and sense of self. In this respect parents have a crucial function to perform throughout their sons' and daughters' childhood, and in their adolescence when offspring should be ready to become more independent from their families. It is by behaving in a reliable and consistent manner that good-enough parents can help their children to differentiate those people and situations that probably could be trusted from those that probably should not be. Young people must learn to discern those likely to be safe from those that may be dangerous; and also to accept that unfortunate mistakes in this assessment are always possible. Failing to put such an important message across can lead either to a paranoid withdrawal from a world only experienced as a place of danger or, at the opposite extreme, mindless exposure to all manner of risk.

What Moodysson shows us in his film, and what we know to be true from the countless episodes of similar abuse we can read about daily in the news, or daily hear about from the couch, is a total failure on the part of Lilya's mother and then of her aunt Anna, as well as of all the men who sexually exploit her, to offer her any care at all, or even to show any concern for her well-being. They leave our fifteen-year old girl to rely on her own inevitably limited resources, vulnerable and alone in a bleak cityscape and decaying social environment where physical and emotional survival would be difficult even for better-equipped adults.

We would expect that the irresponsible behaviour of her relatives and other adults would teach Lilya (Oksana Akinshina) the sad lesson that she should be mistrustful of other people's motives; but in fact she ends up believing those individuals, such as nice-looking, smooth-talking Andrej, who don't think twice about betraying her. Even young Volodya, her only real friend, is aware of, and warns her about, the risks she is putting herself through. How can she be so naive, we wonder? But is her behaviour only due to naiveté or is it also motivated by a profound anger which, because of her past experiences, can only find a distorted expression in self-damaging ways? When Lilya decides to emigrate to Sweden, is there also, hidden somewhere under the conscious wish to improve her condition, an unconscious drive towards self-destructiveness? Evidence for this could be found in Lilya's obvious, if also deeply repressed, need to identify with her mother. The similarity between the two women – both moving abroad with apparently trustworthy men in search of an illusory better life, and in the process abandoning someone younger and emotionally dependent on them – is quite striking.

Moodysson's film portrays with disturbing power the experience of being betrayed by those whom one should instead be able to count on, and the sense of loss that follows such betrayals. Loss is indeed present throughout the film: loss of parents and other benign figures of authority, loss of the friends turning against one, loss of a sense of personal and collective history, loss of whatever sexual innocence Lilya and the other children in the film could have still held on to, loss of a more reliable social environment after the collapse of the old regime and its values.

Was Lilya in any way free, we may ask, to decide to prostitute herself back at home, even before being forced into it by the human traffickers exploiting her through deception and violence? The issue of free will is an age-old insoluble one, debated by, among others, theologians who argue that we can only decide what God wants us to, social scientists for whom what we choose to do with our lives is to a large extent determined by the economic, social and cultural circumstances we find ourselves in, or psychoanalysts who see in their clinical practice the extent to which unconscious motivations prevail over what people consciously believe to be in their best interest.

Was Lilya in any way free, we may again ask, to decide to bring upon herself the ultimate loss, that of her own life? It is tragic that for Lilya, and for her friend Volodya before her, suicide should seem the only available solution when any hope of trust in the world had collapsed. By then, framed Victorian oleographs and dreams of winged angels and the memory of her eleven-year-old loyal friend are no longer enough. Having been the victim of such unspeakable human violence against her, it is only when Lilya leans over the parapet of the bridge overlooking the traffic that, by committing a desperate act of violence against herself, she can assert her own autonomy for the first and last time in her short life.

*****

The first two girls we have encountered in the films discussed in this chapter were young women finding themselves prematurely involved in the seedy world of prostitution: Cabiria just about surviving it, Lilya tragically succumbing to it. The protagonist of *Midnight Cowboy*, male hustler Joe Buck, discovered some meaning in life through his friendship with a social dropout. Our last prostitute, Séverine, is an entirely different character: a middle-class lady who secretly practices the oldest profession as a part-time worker in a Parisian brothel.

Fantasy and reality merge in Luis Buñuel's surrealistic voyage into the mind of Séverine (Catherine Deneuve), a young, beautiful and elegant French lady unhappily married to Pierre (Jean Sorel), a medical doctor. Informed by their friend Monsieur Husson (Michel Piccoli) of the existence of a high-class brothel, she decides after some hesitation to work there as a prostitute during her free afternoon hours. Her job, under the pseudonym of Belle de Jour, in the *maison* efficiently run by Madame Anaïs (Geneviève Page) leads to her tentative experimentations with various perverse sexual practices (from necrophilia to voyeurism, sadomasochism and fetishism), to meet the expectations of her demanding clients. One client is a young criminal named Marcel (Pierre Clementi), with whom she makes the mistake of falling in love.

By 1967, when *Belle de Jour*[8] was released to much critical acclaim and hypocritical expressions of scandalized disbelief, Buñuel had already directed some twenty-six movies. Well-known as he was among film *aficionados*, it was not until *Belle de Jour* that the tide of international mass popularity turned in his favour. Bernardo Bertolucci remembers that Buñuel, who was sitting near him when this movie was presented at the Venice Festival (where it won the Golden Lion), became so anxious that he had to leave the cinema halfway through the screening (personal communication). But, partly because of the explicit (for those days, at least) nature of its subject – a shy and beautiful woman's perverse sexual activities hidden under her bourgeois elegance and discreet respectability – and partly because of the censorial interferences that the film had to endure (not unlike those suffered, and for analogous reasons, by Bertolucci's own *Last Tango in Paris* five years later), *Belle de Jour* turned its nearly septuagenarian auteur into a household name. "It was my biggest commercial success," writes Buñuel in his autobiographical *My Last Breath*, to then add with a hint of false modesty, "which I attribute more to the marvelous whores than to my direction" (Buñuel 1982, p. 243). The theme of prostitution, as we have already mentioned, has been much exploited in the cinema. But we must guess that it is not the sex-for-money aspect of the oldest profession or, *pace* Buñuel, the marvelous bodies of its practitioners to make *Belle de Jour* so unlike anything we have ever seen before, or since.

Let us begin from the beginning – or from the end

Perhaps the horse-drawn coach, with its disturbingly reassuring jingling bells, stands for sexuality and death, the twin pillars of the Gothic component of Romantic tradition, as well as – classically disguised as Eros and Thanatos – of the psychoanalytic edifice itself. Or does its journey through the countryside indicate an uncanny shift away from conscious reality and into a dreamworld of unconscious desires? This would be a twilight space dominated by that same Primary Process mental functioning, disrespectful of the laws of logic and temporality ruling our conscious existence, that also dominates life in the Unconscious, in dreaming, and in moments of creativity and madness. Towards the end of *Belle de Jour*, Séverine, who so often throughout the film looks dissociated and almost lost in a world of her own, tells her husband Pierre: "I don't dream anymore."

Was Séverine's story then, we could ask, just a dream? Was it all a fantasy? We shall never know, anymore than we could find out the contents of the magic box with which its Korean owner provokes the curiosity (fear? excitement?) of the girls in the brothel, while Buñuel uses that same box to provoke our own interest. This withholding of a mystery is similar, by the way, to what also happens when patients in psychoanalysis hint at having just had an interesting fantasy, without however being willing to disclose its content to their therapist. Maybe the box with its intriguing buzzing-bees noise represents the illusion that there is mystery in life until one discovers, usually too late, that there was nothing to be discovered. Indeed, were we to have asked Buñuel himself about it, we would have become one of the countless people ("particularly women," he specifies with a touch of forgivable Latin misogyny) to address him that "senseless" question to which, as he puts it, "since I myself have no idea, I usually reply, 'Whatever you want there to be'" (Buñuel 1982, p. 243). The emperor is naked. The box is empty.[9]

Back to Séverine, we are left intrigued by the issue of fetishism. This issue was already touched upon by Buñuel in the first scene of *El* (1952) and in *The Diary of a Chambermaid* (1964). Fetishism is perhaps the most subtly perverse of all sexual perversions. The classical psychoanalytic interpretation (from Freud's own daring, original and, in the end, surprisingly convincing speculations on this phenomenon) derives from the observation that the little boy cannot quite accept that female human beings, his mother above all, could be anatomically different from himself, for this would evoke in him intolerable castration anxieties. Our boy therefore, when faced with the reality of the female genitals, reacts by denying, or more precisely by disavowing, his perception of this obscure object of his desires and by replacing it with a sort of an hallucination of what he unconsciously wants to believe: that his mother, after all, must have a penis like he does himself.

Interestingly, that same boy would probably use a different defense mechanism, that of rationalization, to explain to himself the lack of a penis he may have noticed in his little sister: "She doesn't have one now because she is still too young, but of course she will grow one later." Either way the intriguing creation in the boy's mind of this imaginary female phallus is likely to cause him problems in adjusting to reality and, as a grownup, in his erotic relationships. A possible solution consists in his replacing this maternal penis with a fetishistic object of his own peculiar choice (perhaps another part of the body, or a shoe, or an item of lingerie) which might originally have been associated in his mind with it. This solution is statistically infrequent, it must be said, at least in its pathological form of a fully fledged sexual perversion. The fetish, then, says Freud in his oft-quoted essay on the subject, is a compromise, a penis turned into something else, "a token of triumph over the threat of castration and a protection against it" (Freud 1927, p. 154). What happens in the end is that "the pervert puts an impersonal object between his desire and his accomplice" (Khan 1979, p. 9).

Two facts are of special interest to us here. The first is that in this famous magic box scene of *Belle de Jour*, the fetishistic object happens to be a container (often the representation of the female genitals) as well as its mysterious content (symbolically, perhaps, a baby in the womb). The second is that such a box, and the perverse fantasy that goes with it, belongs to an Oriental man. Freud, in the article already referred to, uses as an example of the mixed feelings of affection and hostility regularly present in the fetish, "the Chinese custom of mutilating the female foot and then revering it" (Freud 1927, p. 157).

"*Lasciate ogni speranza, o voi che entrate*" (Leave all hope behind, once you have entered here) was the warning engraved on the gateway to Dante's *Inferno*. After an initial resistance to crossing the threshold to the brothel, as if she believed that there could be no return from it, Séverine makes her mind up. Her reasons for attending Madame Anaïs' *maison,* however, remain complex and overdetermined. We would not even dream, of course, of expecting such a filmmaker as Buñuel to offer us a straightforward explanation. We must also rule out without hesitation the suggestion that he puts in the mouth of the impeccably unscrupulous Monsieur Husson: that his friend Séverine does it, like everyone else, just for the money. Her reasons, instead, relate to her need to disappear inside a different mental space – a life of imagination populated by perverse, and therefore repressed, fantasies of degradation – which ironically may feel safer to her than the depressive normality of her social milieu. Or else she prostitutes herself for a deep-seated, unprocessed antagonism against the bourgeois system into which, at the same time, she also fits only too well; like in the flashback scene where, as a child, she rebelled against the priest's expectation that she would take communion. Or maybe we could come to the conclusion that Séverine is discovering in the course of her journey through sexual desires (a sort of an odyssey with a dubious Ithaca at the end of it) that she does not want men to worship her in the way her husband does, and that therefore she attends the *modisterie* as a distraction from her boringly chaste marital life. Or, indeed, her regular frequentation of the brothel could be seen as a sort of unconventional therapeutic journey. Some aspects of that setting (the way in which she is referred to it by Moessieur Husson, the firm but sympathetic understanding she receives from Madame Anaïs, the safe boundaries surrounding its space, its temporal rules, the respect of confidentiality) are all comparable to those also familiar to analytic work. Or, again, her unconventional behaviour may be dictated by a sense of insecurity about her feminine identity, which would then need constant confirmation through the variety of erotic activities she is allowed (indeed, expected) to perform in her free afternoons. This would be consistent with the view that perversions "are as much pathologies of gender-role identity as pathologies of sexuality" (Kaplan 1991, p. 128) insofar as "what makes a perversion a perversion is a mental strategy that employs some social gender stereotypes of masculinity and femininity in a manner that deceives the onlooker about the unconscious meanings of the behaviours she or he is observing" (Kaplan 1991, p. 130). It should be stressed here that uncertainties in the area of gender identity (in this case, whether Séverine feels like a woman) are different from, though not altogether indifferent to, uncertainties in the area of sexual orientation (in this case, whether she feels an attraction for other women). In line with the psychoanalytic belief about a bisexual disposition in all human beings, Séverine's behaviour suggests a conflictual attitude about her sexuality. This attitude is exemplified by her attempt to kiss a reluctant Madame Anaïs (a mother figure) when leaving her workplace for the last time, in contrast with what had happened on her first day there, when she had been the one to turn her face away from Madame's lips. It would be senseless to interpret any sort of heterosexual behaviour, in brothels or anywhere else, as a defense against homoerotic anxieties. However, when heterosexuality takes on a compulsive quality (like, say, in the case of Don Juan) one begins to wonder what latent desires the manifest behaviour may be concealing.

But perhaps Séverine's ultimate reason for becoming a prostitute, if only a part-time one, is simply that she cannot help it. "I am lost," she tells Pierre, "I can't resist." Indeed, it is a mixture of seduction and repulsion that prostitution may hold for any woman in Séverine's position. Catherine Deneuve, only a twenty-two-year-old at the time, hides both reactions behind her magically frosty expression, thus forcing us, the viewers, into the uncomfortable position of having to explore our own fantasies and draw our own moral conclusions.

After her first encounter in Madame Anaïs's *maison*, where she looks and behaves more like a virginal Barbie doll than a real person, Séverine takes a cathartic shower and burns her underwear. She clumsily moves one of her garments to the side of the fireplace, parapraxically leaving behind the evidence of her sexual activities. These will soon include a taste for all sorts of perversions, among them necrophilia with the Duke who, twenty years ahead of the camcorder revolution, places a movie camera in front of his carefully staged incestuous erotic scenario (and in front of Buñuel's own camera).

Another motivation for Séverine may be voyeurism (a theme we will explore in more detail in Chapter Six). Séverine can only let herself visit the brothel wearing dark glasses (the same ones that Pierre, injured in his eyes like an Oedipus who should not see his own murderous and incestuous crimes, will wear after the shooting near the end of the film). She is constantly concerned about being seen, yet she will look through a peephole in the wall at the gynecologist's tragicomedy. In Buñuel's and our own company, the nature of the object of Séverine's voyeuristic activity is a sadomasochistic performance to which, unlike her more experienced colleague, she is herself unable to contribute other

Figure 2.3 Catherine Deneuve in *Belle de Jour* (Buñuel 1967)

than from behind a hole in the wall as an unseen passive spectator. While the scene that we, those other passive spectators, are allowed to watch in identification with Séverine is explicit in all its grotesque physicality, I am reminded of a joke that emphasizes instead the more subtle and paradoxical nature that emotional cruelty can take in such perverse relationships. Being begged by a masochist to *"Please, PLEASE"* really hurt him, a dominatrix looks long and hard at her partner, smiles at him with satisfied contempt and then, triumphantly, replies in a simple *sotto voce*: "I won't." On the surface, of course, the essence of sadomasochistic relationships is power; not only, as is more obvious, on the part of the sadist who can get away with causing pain and humiliation to a consenting partner, but also on the part of the masochist who has the mutually agreed, and consistently respected, authority of putting an end to the game at any time. It is, in other words, the masochist (the gynecologist in *Belle de Jour*) who turns passivity into activity by calling the shots. His mistress, who appears to give the orders, in effect just receives them.

According to Otto Kernberg, "sexual excitement incorporates aggression in the service of love [while] perversity is the recruitment of love in the service of aggression, the consequence of a predominance of hatred over love; its essential expression is the breakdown of boundaries that normally protect the love relationship" (Kernberg 1991, pp. 153–154). However, if we care to look below the surface, we discover that the fascination in such perverse relationships is not so much in the physical or even in the emotional pain which is being caused, or suffered, through this "predominance of hatred over love," but in the artificiality, in the theatricality itself of the scenario being played out. Or, better perhaps, in the tension between the unconscious script and its external actualization, between the fantasies in the minds of its participants and their realization in the outside world. Some psychoanalysts, by the way, would describe the complex ways in which perverse fantasies interact with their enactments, and impinge on one another, as "adaptive and defensive compromise formations that may serve multiple functions" (Fogel 1991, p. 2). Other authors, however, question the very notion of a perverse fantasy on the grounds that there can only be perverse behaviour since all fantasy, by definition, is about the objectionable and the unobtainable (McDougall 1991).

It could be argued that the tension between fantasies and their actualization which I have referred to applies to all sexual relationships, or even to all relationships *tout court*. However, it is precisely the emphasis on the more theatrical aspects of the sadomasochistic game (to the point of almost requiring for its successful accomplishment an imaginary, if not a real, third person as a spectator) that distinguishes it and other such perverse games from other intimate rapports. This theatricality connotes its extremely limited, almost claustrophobic nature, whereby the experiential range of feelings and sensations is reduced to the compulsive repetition of an almost identical pattern of stimuli followed by an almost identical pattern of responses, ad libitum. What from behind Madame Anaïs's peephole can look like an exciting erotic comedy, from the participants' viewpoint can ultimately only feel like a depressing tragedy.

We may wonder whether Freud's original seduction theory (according to which adult neurotic symptoms are caused by childhood sexual abuse) may also, or even better, apply to perversions inasmuch as these are, in his own words, the "negative of neurosis" (Freud 1905, p. 165). Modern psychoanalysis tends to locate the psychogenesis of perversions in early traumatic experiences. For instance, Glasser (1986) has identified what he calls a *Core Complex*, characterized by a tension between dread and fascination for a sort of "black hole" associated with a powerful pulling back towards the mother's body.[10] According to Cooper, "the core trauma . . . is the experience of terrifying passivity in relation to the preoedipal mother perceived as dangerously malignant. . . . The development of a perversion is a miscarried repair of this injury, basically through dehumanization of the body" (Cooper 1991, p. 23).

Séverine's flashback memory of sexual molestation when she was a young girl is paralleled in the present by the brothel's chambermaid's daughter, who seems doomed, after finishing her studies, to become herself a whore. Séverine's flashback is exorcised by being replayed again and again *chez* Madame Anaïs. Relevant in this respect is the view that "perversion, the erotic form of hatred, . . . serves to convert childhood trauma to adult triumph" (Stoller 1975, quoted in Fogel and Myers 1991, p. 36). Also relevant is Chasseguet-Smirgel's (1983) theory that perversions result from a confusion, taking place in the early years of development and often encouraged by adults, between the genders and between the generations, so that a girl may be expected to fantasize that her own sexual body includes the male genitals, or to behave towards her father as if she were his wife.

If there is a schizoid split between the bourgeois order of Séverine's marital relationship (or lack thereof), skiing holidays, dinner parties with friends and games at the tennis club, on the one hand, and the deviant, perverse, disruptive sexual depravity of her afternoons in the brothel on the other, at the same time there is, I would like to suggest, a striking continuity between these two apparently contrasting worlds. Séverine's (and Deneuve's) austere elegance, mirrored in the formal coolness of Buñuel's *mise-en-scène* and of Sacha Vierny's photography, fits as easily in the sordid ambiance of Madame Anaïs's establishment as corruption and hypocrisy belong to Séverine's middle-class existence. We could speculate that the house of prostitution as the metaphoric antithesis of marriage has the unconscious function of keeping the latter alive and, with it, the normality it symbolizes. After all, as McDougall points out, "most sexual perversions . . . are attempts to achieve and maintain a heterosexual relationship" (McDougall 1991, p. 190). The link, the go-between, the *trait d'union* is Monsieur Husson. Belonging more than Séverine does to both worlds almost by nature, he concretely crosses the boundaries between them by coming into the brothel, by contemptuously leaving Belle de Jour as payment some money to buy chocolates for Pierre, and finally by revealing to him what his wife is up to every afternoon between two and five o'clock. A reference perhaps, this last one, to Mrs Alice Ford's free hour for Falstaff's visit "between ten and eleven" (or, in Arrigo Boito's libretto for Verdi's opera, *"dalle due alle tre"*). Like in ancient Rome, where *Semel in anno licet insanire* (once a year, that is *only* once a year for Carnival, doing crazy things is allowed), such a temporal restriction, and indeed the whole mostly unspoken set of rules regulating life in the house of prostitution, provides a containment to the dangers represented by sexual deviancy. In other words, it is the presence of such boundaries that allows behaviour disruptive of the social order to occur without spilling over into madness or into tragedy – which is of course precisely what happens when Marcel forces them to be trespassed. Indeed, Séverine's emotional involvement with Marcel is by far more threatening to her psychological equilibrium and fragile marriage to Pierre than either her asexual behaviour as Séverine in the marital bedroom, or her sexual one as Belle de Jour in the brothel.

Let us end at the end – or at the beginning. Perhaps the horse-drawn coach with its disturbingly reassuring jingling bells indicates that everything we have seen projected on the screen was but a dream all along; that fantasy and reality, like desire and its fulfillment, draw their raison d'être from each other and always merge. And that works of art, a good film for instance, have the function of reminding us that they are ultimately indistinguishable.

Notes

1. The Italian translation of the word *pimp* is *sfruttatore* (literally: *exploiter*). No room for ambiguities there.
2. "Midnight cowboy" is a slang expression for prostitution. Analogously the title of Luis Buñuel's *Belle de Jour* paraphrases the description of *Belle de Nuit* given in France to prostitutes.
3. The topic of adult male friendships, incidentally, is one described in a number of good films – such as *Of Mice and Men* (Milestone 1939), *The Odd Couple* (Saks 1968) and *Distant [Uzak]* (Ceylan 2002) – but surprisingly little explored in psychoanalytic writings.
4. Perhaps Freud was making an indirect reference to prostitution when he remarked that "money matters are treated by civilized people in the same way as sexual matters – with the same inconsistency, prudishness and hypocrisy" (Freud 1913c, p. 131).
5. *Cabiria [Le notti di Cabiria]* (Italy 1956). Directed by Federico Fellini. Written by Federico Fellini, Ennio Flaiano and Tullio Pinelli. Starring Giulietta Masina (Cabiria), Amedeo Nazzari (Alberto Lazzari), and Francois Perier (Oscar D'Onofrio).
6. In Chapter 5 I have expanded on the concept of rescue fantasies in my interpretation of *Amores Perros* (Iñarritu 2000) and referred to it in relation to *Vertigo* (Hitchcock 1958).
7. *Lilya-4-Ever* (Sweden 2002). Directed and written by Lukas Moodysson. Starring Oksana Akinshina (Lilya), Artyom Bogucharsky (Volodya), and Pavel Panomaryov (Andrei).
8. *Belle de Jour* (France 1967). Director Luis Buñuel. Writer Luis Buñuel, from Joseph Kessel's novel. Starring Catherine Deneuve (Sévérine), Jean Sorel (Pierre), Michel Piccoli (Husson), Geneviève Page (Madame Anaïs), and Pierre Clementi (Marcel).
9. It is empty unlike, by the way, another famous and rather larger box to be spotted on the silver screen: the one the content of which the Coen brothers – who could be counted among Buñuel's own many adoptive sons – also do not share with the viewers of their

Barton Fink (1991). In their case, however, the box looks quite heavy. It is about the same size as the one in the terrific final scene of David Fincher's *Seven* (1995), which we do know contained a severed head.

10. I have argued that these psychodynamics are also fundamental to the personality and behaviour of such film characters as Scottie in Hitchcock's *Vertigo* (1958), dominated as they are by an internal conflict consisting of a magnetic pull toward a deadly trap (see Chapter Five).

Chapter 3

The young ones

Films on children

Since the dawn of our discipline at the end of the nineteenth century, and in particular since the publication of the *Three essays on the theory of sexuality* (Freud 1905) and of the Little Hans case history (Freud 1909), the psychoanalytic edifice has been founded on its understanding of child development. Psychoanalysts believe in the core importance of early-life experiences, both the good-enough ones allowing for a healthy development within a facilitating environment and the negative ones that can interfere with such development; the latter may be caused by traumatic events, early losses, abuse or neglect, with consequences that may continue throughout life. We may forget, repress or distort our past, but we cannot prevent it from marking us, for better or for worse, for the rest of our days, nor from affecting to some extent even the next generations.

Thanks to the seminal contributions of such pioneers of child analysis as Anna Freud, Melanie Klein, Erik Erikson, Donald Winnicott and Margaret Mahler, to only mention a few, our knowledge about the internal world of children, about their fantasies and dreams, about the meaning of their games and the psychodynamics of their object relationships has expanded, with major theoretical and clinical implications for our practice in relation also to adolescents and adults, as well as to the children themselves.

Given then the importance of childhood for our discipline, it seems appropriate in the context of this book that we should focus on how characters of only a few years of age have been represented on the screen. Throughout the history of cinema and all over the world, filmmakers have been successfully working with children, thus challenging the myth that it is too risky to make movies with them (or with animals). This work has produced a large number of feature films (some of them, but certainly not all, also intended for a young audience) with children and adolescents as protagonists. It must be said that the majority of these films simply reproduce, and in the process also reinforce, the most trite stereotypes about children. Others though, such as the films included in this chapter on younger children and in the next one on adolescents, show considerable insight and understanding about their characters' emotional life, and the inner conflicts and external predicaments they have to face. The best of these films have succeeded in portraying with intelligence and sensitivity the internal world of children and adolescents, their relationships with each other and with adults, their capacity to play and have fun, their sense of humour, and their suffering during hard times. These movies speak the same language as their young characters.[1]

Last but not least, it may be worth noting that what filmmakers and other artists do in their work when it consists of inventing characters, creating magic objects and making up entire new scenarios bears a similarity to children's own imaginative play. In fact the former originates from, and is an organic development of, the latter. In other words there is a continuity between the imaginative play of children and the creative work of artists, filmmakers included.

*****

"As film-makers we're not there to order people around; we're there to listen, to absorb, and to try to draw people out and serve them. And, as far as we could, that's what we did on Kes." (Ken Loach, in Fuller 1998, p. 43)

Ken Loach's *Kes*[2] is one of the classic British films about children. It was shot at the school in Barnsley, in Yorkshire, where Barry Hines was a teacher. Hines was the author of the novel *A Kestrel for a Knave* (1968), on which the film is based, and Loach's frequent collaborator. "The reason we only went to one classroom in one school in Barnsley to pick a boy for *Kes*," states Loach, "was part of the thinking behind the project, the idea being that there's a kid in every class like Billy" (in Fuller 1998, p. 114).

Kes, which unlike many other Loach films was successful at the box office, marks a shift in style by placing the camera in the position of the observer and by giving the viewers more time and space to reflect on what they are watching. The movie was influenced, through Chris Menges' photography, by Czech cinema: "A conscious move away from newsreely, chasing kind of photography to a more reflective, observed, sympathetically lit style of photography" (Loach, in Fuller 1998, p. 39).

Billy Casper, played by the much younger-looking fifteen-year-old David Bradley, is a boy growing up in a dysfunctional family and attending a dysfunctional school in a Yorkshire village. Introverted by nature and bullied by society, Billy finds some comfort, plus a mixture of admiration and envy from the other schoolboys, as he manages to tame a kestrel who becomes his only friend. Bill's kestrel soon turns into the target of projections of his own wishful fantasies of freedom from the unhappy future to which he is condemned by his social condition.

Billy, and millions of other boys and girls like him, should expect from society to be trained, not tamed the way his school tries to tame him, and the way he in turn seeks to tame his bird of prey. But, as *Kes* shows us, children are consistently being let down because institutions often fail to help the very people they are set up to serve. This failure is a common theme in Loach's films, whether he looks at trade unions, social services, political parties, or families. We watch Billy being let down not just by the school or the Youth Employment office but even, in its small way, by the *public* library that creates unnecessary bureaucratic problems

Figure 3.1 David Bradley in *Kes* (Loach 1969)

for him, thus pushing him to steal from the *private* bookshop the volume he needed in order to learn the noble art of falconry.

Loach has an eye for Laingian double binds. He had already directed the television play *In Two Minds* (1967) and his next film, *Family Life* (1969), would concern the abuses of conventional psychiatry. He has the girl at assembly read the Parable of the Stray Sheep only minutes before a child, selected at random among a hundred, gets punished for coughing.

In Loach's filmic universe even minor characters and their motivations can be intriguingly complex. It would be too easy to see Billy's older brother Jud ("*our* Jud") as just a bully "too big for his boots," as his mother tells him. Instead we are constantly reminded that Jud too is a victim, that he has probably been bullied himself, and that he has to spend his days down a coal-pit. When Billy, after his bird is killed, tells Jud, "You could have taken it out on me," I think of how often the target of someone's anger (or sadism, or envy) is displaced either onto someone else, or onto an object belonging to him or her. I am reminded here of Freud's comment, when the Nazis burnt his books in a Vienna square, that he was lucky he was not living in the Middle Ages, for then they would have burnt him instead. Little he knew that, had he lived only a few more years, this is precisely what the Nazis could have done to him, and what they did do to his four elderly sisters and to millions of others.

The protagonist of the story is himself far from being an entirely positive hero; and we must be grateful to Loach for that. Billy is cheeky with his teachers and with the librarian ("I am twenty-one! I vote!" he lies). He tries to trip the stationer over and he steals whenever he has got a chance (comic books from his employer, eggs and milk from the milkman, the bet money from his brother whom he insults whenever he can, the book on falconry from the bookshop). Further, Billy is the boy who holds an innocent younger child round his neck when the bullies plant a pack of cigarettes on him. In other words Billy has learned, and it is a sad lesson, to treat others in a similar way as they treat him – a situation we encounter again and again also in our analytic work with patients. We may wonder whether a present-day Billy would still try to survive his alienating environment by training a kestrel in the fields, or withdraw indoors instead to play violent computer games.

In the film Billy's parents are absent. The mother is physically there but too preoccupied with her own problems to ever get adequately involved with her sons. The missing father is replaced by a bossy, persecutory older brother and by a series of teachers who do not listen to their students. The exception is Mr Farthing, the delightful character who is genuinely concerned about his pupils' difficulties but who feels himself rather powerless to bring about any change; the best he can do under the circumstances is to show some understanding and kindness. I imagine Loach must have identified with him and his predicament.[3]

If I now let myself free-associate for a few minutes, an activity not unknown to those involved with psychoanalysis, I am reminded of a very different relationship between a boy and a bird of prey in an episode involving an early childhood frightening memory: "While I was in my cradle a vulture came down to me, and opened my mouth with its tail, and struck me many times with its tail against my lips." The child in question is Leonardo da Vinci. The childhood memory, reported in his *Scientific Notebooks*, is the subject of a detailed biographical study by Freud (1910a) who interpreted it as a later fantasy and related it to Leonardo's ambiguous sexual orientation. The bird in question was actually a *kite* (a *nibio* in Leonardo's Italian) – a member of the falcon's family more similar to a kestrel such as the one trained by Billy in Loach's film than it is to the "vulture" we find in Freud's erroneous translation.

And speaking of kites, if I am allowed to indulge in some further free associations, I remember my excitement many years ago of flying for the first time a (paper) kite on Hampstead Heath, of feeling those light oscillations in the strength and direction of the wind amplified inside my body. The kite for me, and perhaps the kestrel for Billy, became then a sort of appendix in the sky, the centre of an always uncertain relationship with the world out there. Its fascination may rest on this very uncertainty. Our wish is to bring back to earth that part of ourselves which for a brief moment had dared to explore, beyond our bodies, the depths of the sky. That wish is complemented by the wish to let the kite, or the kestrel, go free – and, carried by its light wings, to let ourselves go free with it.

*****

Written and directed by Victor Erice in 1973, *The Spirit of the Beehive*[4] was aptly described by a critic as "a visually poetic, haunting, allegorical film on innocence, illusion, and isolation." The film was acclaimed internationally as a masterpiece and won several major awards.

The indirect influence of a psychoanalytic approach to filmmaking is made explicit by Erice himself when, in relation to this work, he states: "I believe in the less conscious (in other words, the subconscious or unconscious) experiences and feelings that gradually build up in our minds without our being too aware of them. The problem in art isn't just to have ideas, but how to express them and give them body and life."

The Spirit of the Beehive describes two young girls, Isabel and Ana, growing up in the Spanish countryside soon after the end of the Civil War, as they experience a mixture of shock, excitement and curiosity after watching James Whale's classic horror movie *Frankenstein* (1931) in their village. This stimulates them to fantasize about the monster and how they could get in contact with him, while their parents remain mostly indifferent to what goes on in their daughters' inner world.

Human beings have always attempted to cope with the anxieties stemming from their limitations – physical, emotional, mental and otherwise – by imagining worlds where such shortcomings are magically denied or overcome. Their impotence is thus transformed into omnipotence, their ignorance into omniscience, their mortality into eternal life, their unhappiness on earth into bliss in heaven. We learn from psychoanalytic developmental theories that the origins of such grandiose fantasies may be traced back to the infants' primary narcissism and to their belief that the mother's breast (concretely and metaphorically speaking) will always be available on demand – a certainty to be challenged early enough, of course, by the disturbing intrusion into the child's life of the Reality Principle. Mythologies, including those that take the form of religions, are but variations on the theme of such primitive wishes and are to be found in all cultures.

In the *Zeitgeist* of the nineteenth century, characterized as it was by its emphasis on scientific progress, one of these myths found special fortunes: it consists in the wish to artificially recreate human life by removing various organs from corpses, assembling them into one body, and then infusing a sparkle of life into it, perhaps with the help of magnetic energy or of the then newly discovered electricity. Not unlike those arrogant, if also brave, biblical builders of the Tower of Babel who hoped to get close to God with their construction, any woodcarver à la Mastro Geppetto (Pinocchio's father in Carlo Collodi's 1883 masterpiece) or any scientist à la doctor Henry Frankenstein could learn to imitate, and thus to challenge, God's (or rather Mother Nature's) powers to form new lives. Dr. Frankenstein's enterprise was doomed to a tragic outcome in Mary Shelley's 1818 genial literary creation, and also in James Whale's film. Whales gave nineteenth-century science a scary visual representation in 1931, but perhaps this would seem less outlandishly fantastic in our own technologically dominated third millennium, when the creation of artificial intelligence, of anthropomorphic robots, and of cloned sheep is fast moving from the realm of science fiction to that of ordinary reality.

"I had received a proposal to make a film on the theme of Frankenstein, but actually in that horror genre," explained Victor Erice about the genesis of *The*

Spirit of the Beehive, "but when I started to do the budget, chance happily intervened in my favour because that kind of film needs a lot of sets and famous actors, and the producer had to admit he didn't have quite enough funds. So when I proposed a Spanish version of Frankenstein – not quite so extravagant, without big sets and with only four weeks of filming – he liked the idea. . . . On my work desk I had cut out a picture, a frame from James Whale's *Frankenstein,* that moment when the monster and the child are together. . . . I understood that in that image everything was contained. I called on my personal experiences and decided that the identification with the child and the film would be far greater if the child was a girl and not a boy. And so gradually the story started unfolding" (Erice in Geoff Andrew's BFI interview, September 2003).

We can well believe that, in the imagination of young children growing up in a village in 1940, the sight of Boris Karloff in the role of doctor Frankenstein's monster, projected on an improvised screen in their village town-hall, must have been truly scary. The "word of friendly warning" offered by the presenter of the film claiming that its story "is not to be taken too seriously" must have done little to assuage these children's fears. We encounter the two protagonists of our film – seven-year old Ana (Ana Torrent) and her elder sister Isabel (Isabel Tellería) – unable to fall asleep after the screening of *Frankenstein,* their minds still full of the disturbing images they have been watching. How could children like them respond emotionally to such distressing material? How would they conceptualize and integrate it within their mental space? Would their reactions, as girls of latency period age, be substantially different from those of boys, or of older children, or even of adults, when being presented with a monstrous creature walking about a scientist's laboratory? A monster who then throws a young girl like themselves into the lake as if she were just another marigold? Ana and Isabel know that what they had seen was *just* a film ("In the movies it's all fake, it's a trick," says the older girl), much as we know that Victor Erice's is also just a film. Yet, beyond all rationalizations, they must have found it impossible to keep its fictional reality entirely separate from their daily experiences, and to understand it as nothing more than the product of someone else's imagination with the help of a few good film tricks. Such, by the way, is the power and indeed the fascination of cinema for us all.

In the poignant scene of their *sotto voce* dialogue in bed, we hear sleepy Isabel trying to answer her wide-eyed younger sister's questions by making her believe that she, Isabel, knows more than she actually does about such things as monsters, ghosts and spirits. "I saw him alive," she claims. "Where?" Ana inquires. "In a place I know near the village. People can't see him. He only goes out at night." "Is he a ghost?" "No, he's a spirit." In another scene, Isabel pretends to be dead and then, in the dressed-up guise of a monster, creeps up on Ana from behind, almost enjoying scaring her. We presume this is a way to deal with her own fears through the well-known defensive mechanism of identification with the aggressor. Ana, on her part, who earlier on was not much convinced by Isabel's parapsychological explanations about ghosts and spirits, is not too frightened now by her sister's dramatic performance. However, Ana will still pursue her wish to meet the monster, who she believes can make itself visible at the bottom of the well near an abandoned farm, albeit only as a ghostly apparition. But, we may ask, what are Ana and Isabel really looking for? We must assume that in their solitary search for the monster's spirit, alongside experiencing some sense of adventure and excitement, they secretly hope to come across someone who could offer them the understanding and affection which neither of their rather absent parents could be trusted to give them. They wanted to find someone sufficiently in touch with their inner world and sympathetic to their insoluble existential dilemmas about good and evil, life and death, bodies and sexuality (questions that all children have to struggle with) to help them dispel or at least reduce their anxieties.

Indeed, these girls' parents seem not just to ignore each other, but also to be quite indifferent to their daughters. Teresa is busy writing letters to a former lover living in France, while "misanthropic" Fernando (Teresa's definition of her husband) is obsessed with the meticulous observation of bees. The imagery of the beehive, by the way, repeated in the hexagonal pattern on the house windowpanes, creates in the film what a critic described as "a pervasive sense of claustrophobia and geographic disconnection." The girls are often left by themselves. They play dangerous games on the railway lines and wander in the open countryside as if they didn't need any parental supervision. On a couple of occasions, it is true, we witness Fernando and Teresa behaving like good-enough parents. The girls' father takes them out to pick mushrooms and explains the difference between the edible and the poisonous ones – perhaps an indirect lesson in moral values. In another scene, Teresa affectionately combs Ana's hair and tries to answer her questions about spirits ("A spirit is a spirit," she says – hardly an enlightening explanation!) followed, moreover, by the instruction to be a good girl, but also by a genuinely tender hug. Later, when Ana runs away and cannot be found anywhere for a few hours, both Teresa and Fernando are clearly upset, though maybe also out of guilt for not having taken proper care of her. All in all, one is left with the impression that these parents are not engaged with their daughters in an emotionally profound and consistent way, and that therefore these still very young and needy children cannot quite rely on them. It is significant that when Ana is worried about what could have happened to her sister, she goes to the more present and caring servant Milagros for help, and not to her mother.

A delightful scene in *The Spirit of the Beehive* is the one that takes place in the classroom, where a well-meaning teacher gives a rudimentary anatomy lesson to her pupils by making them reassemble, Frankenstein-like, the different organs (heart, lungs, stomach, eyes – no genitals, of course) on a wooden mannequin named Don José. It is as if such whole objects as human beings were just the sum total of the part objects they contain; a theme incidentally also touched on by another Spanish filmmaker, Pedro Almodóvar, in his recent movie *The Skin I Live In* (2011), again inspired by the Frankenstein story.

In *The Spirit of the Beehive*, as well as throughout the rest of director Erice's scanty filmic production, we can perceive the noisy presence of time ticking by:

a theme visually illustrated here by the father's musical watch, an album of old family photographs, the cycle of the bees' lives, the children's daily ritual walk to and from school. "Films are obviously full of time," Erice remarked; "all forms of art have expressed time in one way or another. But none has managed to contain it, as a bowl would contain water, as film has managed to do."

A repeated image in *The Spirit of the Beehive* is that of fire. Matches, candles, cigarettes, bonfires and oil lamps are here symbols not only of cathartic purification, but also perhaps of the destructive powers of conflict. At one level the film could be interpreted as an allegory of Spain at the tail end of its bloody Civil War – a country first traumatized, and then for the following four decades anaesthetized, by the presence of a monstrous dictatorship. The literary and filmic Frankenstein and the historical Franco can be seen as two men affected by a similar delusion of omnipotence: the former to imitate God by creating life through a perverted use of science, the latter to oppress his country through his violent and authoritarian regime (Erice's film was released two years before the end of Franco's long dictatorship). Yet, *The Spirit of the Beehive* may as well be set in any place and at any time. Unfolding at a slow tempo, Erice's film allows us to immerse ourselves in the two children's fantasy world and magical thinking, skillfully explored by the filmmaker's camera as it flawlessly moves in and out of the family's comfortable country house. I was intrigued to learn that the film is made up of exactly 500 indoor and 500 outdoor shots, almost to assert the presence in the children's lives of a perfect balance between subjective experiences and external reality.

Alongside more joyful, light-hearted and playful moments in the girls' existence, we will not find it surprising that their imagination should also be populated by primitive fears of dying. After all, the mind of children is, not unlike cinema

Figure 3.2 Ana Torrent in *The Spirit of the Beehive* (Erice 1973)

itself, a contradictory juxtaposition of lights and shadows. Stimulated both by the fictions of horror cinema and by the realities of horror history, we hear much talking of spirits and ghosts, we see religious icons of skulls and crucifixions, and we watch Isabel attempting to strangle the cat or pretending to lie dead herself. We even come across a corpse – real rather than imagined this time, if still within the fictional world of the film – of a Republican soldier (perhaps the mysterious recipient of Teresa's love letters?) shot by Franco's army in an abandoned barn. When he was still alive but injured and in hiding, Ana had offered him an apple with a similar innocent generosity to the one of little girl Maria toward Franken-stein's monster. We assume Ana offers the apple in identification with Maria and with the unconscious hope to rewrite that frightening story and survive where Maria had succumbed. Covered by a blanket, the Partisan's body will be dis-played in the town-hall makeshift mortuary, in the very same room where, earlier in the film, the villagers had been watching *Frankenstein*.

A critic described *The Spirit of the Beehive* as "a haunting mood piece that dispenses with plot, and works its spells through intricate patterns of sound and image." I am aware that it may feel difficult for some viewers to relate to films such as this which, like those of such great directors as Jean Vigo and Yasujiro Ozu, lack a conventional, straightforward narrative. However, I believe that the deliberate absence of a recognizable plot is here abundantly made up for by the filmmaker's lyrical emphasis on atmosphere, by the powerful visual impact of its simple yet always beautiful photography and, most of all, by the accuracy with which the two little girls' inner world – whether excited by curiosity, delighted with their discoveries, or tormented by anxiety – is represented in the film, allow-ing us to identify with the characters and reminding us of what it was like for us, too, to be children.

*****

Ana Torrent, the young actress who at the age of seven had given such an impressive performance as Ana in *The Spirit of the Beehive,* would three years later be Ana again in another masterpiece of Spanish cinema that centers on closely observed children, *Cría Cuervos.*[5]

Directed, written and produced by Carlos Saura, *Cría Cuervos* revolves around a young girl's tragically painful encounters with death.[6] The film has an appar-ently straightforward narrative (a girl, Ana, deludes herself that she has poisoned her father, whom she blames for the death of her beloved mother). Beyond the narrative, however, the film displays a complex structure reflecting a multilayered allegorical exploration of middle-class secrets and lies, Spanish contemporary politics, genuine as well as hypocritical family relationships, and existential pre-occupations about the human condition.

Here I shall focus my comments on Saura's acute perception of the children's minds: their emotional life, their sufferings and joys, their constructions of what surrounds them and their understanding of the bizarre and often insensitive world of adults, who deny unpleasant realities by calling them lies or dreams. It is difficult to think of other films with such a sympathetic, unhurried and uncompromising insight into the private world of childhood. Furthermore, few other male film-makers (Ingmar Bergman is one of them, François Truffaut another) have such a deep understanding of women and their internal worlds as Carlos Saura. In fact everyone in *Cría Cuervos* belongs to the female gender, three generations of them: Ana and her sisters Irene and Maite, their mother (played by Geraldine Chaplin, Saura's own wife), their aunt, grandmother, and housekeeper, as well as the more detached observer Ana as a young woman (also played by Chaplin). The few men in the film are marginal characters, only functional to the exploration of the women's psychology.

With a sparse use of flashbacks and flashforwards locating the present in a wider historical context, the narrative revolves around the dynamics of a bour-geois family literally collapsing under a veneer of normality and good table man-ners. This family is not dissimilar from those so sarcastically targeted by the surrealistic camera of Luis Buñuel (from whose work Saura likes to quote). Little Ana, the middle child with razor-sharp beautiful eyes, sees through it all. As a critic commented, "Saura has succeeded in showing us the inside of childhood. One has to be a great artist to be able to reflect the true feelings of a child thrown in the turmoil of life. Little Ana's eyes are a world of suffering, of understanding, of emotions. This child has seen death, she has known it directly and she has no fear. Either to experience it or to give it or to see it."

With her words Ana cuts deep inside those who surround her. She is engaged in an unrelenting search for their hidden truths, and she accepts no compromise. She refuses, unlike her sisters, to conform to the false ritual of kissing her dead father in his coffin. She demands to see the generous breasts of the housemaid Rosa, who appears to conceal within them the answer to so many mysteries. She does not refrain from telling those she hates that she wants them to die. Indeed, hav-ing become herself quietly obsessed with death (both its reality and fantasy, both her own and that of others), Ana has no hesitation about murdering (or, at least, omnipotently convincing herself she can) anyone whom she believes deserves to die: her father, whom she considers responsible for his wife's illness and death; her grandmother, whom she knows has already lived long enough and gets little pleasure out of her constrained existence; her aunt, whom she sees as the usurper of her mother's place in the house. But poison-laced drinks, as Ana discovers, do not always work, and the loaded gun inherited from her military father is promptly taken away from her hands.

I would now like to focus on a four-minute-long scene in *Cría Cuervos* which I find extraordinarily powerful and meaningful. It follows a sequence where Rosa, who has just impressed Ana by showing off her breasts, encourages her to answer the grandmother's insistent bell-call: "See what that witch wants!" Rosa tells the girl. (The grandmother had earlier been referred to as "a nuisance.") Ana is a child who does not say much, but has seen and heard everything: physical pain, sex, betrayal and, most of all, death. Yet she seems to be the only character in the film who loves the elderly lady. Having suffered a stroke, the grandmother still looks aristocratically elegant, but is paralyzed in a wheelchair and can only communicate nonverbally by nodding or moving her head from side to side, and by smiling or frowning. The close encounter between Ana and her grandmother takes place in front of a wall covered with old photographs and postcards pinned to a board, the visible and tangible representation of memories. We, the viewers, are now the privileged witnesses to a profoundly intimate exchange, suspended, not unlike the psychoanalytic relationship itself, somewhere between a monologue and a dialogue. Ana's grandmother is bored with life and lost in a whole nostalgic world of her own, matched by the equally nostalgic background melody of "Mary Cruz," a famous Spanish song.

To entertain her, the child plays what is probably a familiar game between them. She points to the pictures on the wall: "This? This one then? Do you want to see it closer?" While the camera moves backwards and forwards in close-ups, the girl inquires about their content: "Who is it? Mama? If it isn't Mama, who can it be? Who then? Your mother? A friend?" But Ana not only has something to learn about the past from her grandmother; she also helps her to remember what the images represent by quoting back to the old lady sentences she herself must have heard many times before: "The postcard of the lake. You were in Switzerland with Grandfather when you were young, and this hotel reminds you of your honeymoon. At dawn the lake was beautiful, full of swans. You could see the snow-covered mountains. And this window was the window of your room." The range and intensity of emotions in the facial expressions of both the girl and her grandmother during this sequence is astonishingly moving.

Then Ana gets closer, takes her grandmother's hand in her own and affectionately caresses her. She can see the great sadness in the old woman's eyes – almost

Figure 3.3 Ana Torrent in *Cría Cuervos* (Saura 1976)

a reflection of her own. Concerned as she is herself with thoughts about death, she asks in a chillingly natural, matter-of-fact way (and it is almost a statement): "You want to die? Do you want me to help you to die?" As the lady seems to nod, Ana leaves. "I'll be right back," she says, and soon returns with her secret, omnipotent weapon, which she believed had already been effective once before. "Look," she says, "it's a terrible poison. With one spoonful of this powder you can kill an elephant. Yes, a terrible poison, lethal." But the grandmother now hesitates. She shakes her head, and Ana respectfully inquires: "No? You don't want it? But before you told me you did. No? Why not?" Ana had not asked her father's consent before poisoning him, or believing to do so, with the justification that he had betrayed, in more ways than one, his wife, and therefore also herself, his daughter. Nor will she ask for her Aunt Paulina's consent later in the film. (Paulina inadequately tries to take her dead sister's place, to the point of using the very same words to tell the children the same fairy tales they used to hear from their mother.) At the point of the grandmother's refusal, Ana puts the lid back on her magic powder; we do not know whether she is feeling more disappointed or relieved. "As you like," she calmly tells her grandmother.

In these four masterful minutes of film, Saura gives us, and it is like a wonderful present to his viewers, a precious insight into our contrasting wishes to remember and to forget. Through Saura, we peer into the special rapport that can develop between children and old people, into the depths of human tenderness and, above all, into our desperate need to communicate with one another.

*****

Another Spanish girl, only a couple of years older than the Ana of *Cría Cuervos,* is the protagonist of *Pan's Labyrinth.*[7] This is a film written, directed and coproduced by Guillermo del Toro. It is set in the same period of Spanish turbulent history as *The Spirit of the Beehive,* and like that film it has as its protagonist a young girl lost between her vivid imagination and the horrors of war. In its original Spanish title, *El labirinto del Fauno,* the word *faun* refers to the forest spirit, half human and half goat, of Roman mythology, while *labyrinth* refers to the Greek legend of Theseus and the Minotaur: a mythical place where, as a character in the film warns its young protagonist, "one can easily get lost."

The film is set in 1944 at the tail end of the Spanish Civil War. It stars the twelve-year-old Spanish actress Ivana Baquero as Ofelia, a sweet but sad girl who has suffered the loss of her father, is poorly understood by her pregnant mother, and is constantly on the verge of being abused by a psychopathic stepfather. This man, an army captain determined to destroy those still resisting the dictatorial regime of Francisco Franco, is played by Sergi López, a most versatile Catalan actor whom we have had occasion to admire in both romantic roles (Fonteyne's *A Pornographic Affair* 1999, see Chapter Five) and in vicious ones (Moll's *With a Friend Like Harry . . .* [2000] and Frears's *Dirty Pretty Things* [2002]).

Photographed like del Toro's other films by Guillermo Navarro in a rich palette of colours and lights, sumptuously designed by art director Eugenio Caballero (both of them Oscar-winners), and displaying a battery of impressive yet unobtrusive special effects, *Pan's Labyrinth* could be described as a Gothic fairy tale, or as a horror fantasy, or as the nightmare of a girl struggling to survive in a hostile environment, or as the filmic equivalent of the magic realism of some Latin American literature, or even as a war movie. In fact, trying to pigeonhole *Pan's Labyrinth* within any of the classical film genres would prove both impossible and unfair. Ultimately, this is just a del Toro movie – a true auteur's own original and impressive contribution to world cinema.[8]

The boundaries between the internal and external world, between fantasy and reality, and between conscious and unconscious functioning, are often less clear-cut than we think. When they disappear altogether we are faced with a psychotic condition, but psychotic states of mind such as dreams as well as much of our daytime mental activity (given its mostly oneiric quality) belong to our normal life and do not constitute symptoms of psychopathology. At the same time a sharp cut, or split, between different realities can occur whereby one mental universe is created in order to avoid facing the other, which is then denied whenever the latter would be experienced as unacceptable or unbearable. This is frequently the case, for instance, in victims of abuse and in individuals who have suffered major losses.

The artistic medium of cinema lends itself well to the representation of different layers of reality within the same work, transporting its audiences in and out of them. Indeed we could think of cinema as a sort of bridge through which we are invited to move, smoothly at times, forcefully at others, across different realities. On the surface, documentaries seem to provide an objective representation of the external world, while fictional features create a completely imaginary one. These extremes, however, are only caricatures of the truth, for in fact both kinds of film share in a complex, though often barely definable, admixture of both worlds. If then the representation of this concoction of various levels of reality applies to a certain extent to all movies, it is also the case that it does so in a more intentional way only to some of them. Some filmmakers (such as Jan Svankmajer and David Cronenberg) have focused their artistic skills on deliberately portraying contrasting worlds – some recognizable as objectively and historically *real*, others as undoubtedly *fantastic* – and then establishing links, throwing bridges, or emphasizing conflicts between them. For their viewers the experience can be confusing and disturbing.

Del Toro is a master in this art. His *Pan's Labyrinth*, as well as his earlier *Cronos* (1993) and *The Devil's Backbone* (2001), intrigue and fascinate us precisely because they draw their audiences into identifying with characters who find themselves moving in and out of different layers of reality. This effect, as Roger Ebert clarifies in his review of *Pan's Labyrinth*, "is achieved with consummate skill by its filmmakers through a moving foreground wipe – an area of darkness, or a wall or a tree that wipes out the military [the "real" world] and wipes in the labyrinth [the realm of "fantasy"], or vice versa. This technique [of using vertical wipes] insists that his two worlds are not intercut, but live in edges of the same frame" (Ebert 2007). It is in that space ("in edges of the same frame") where they at first enter into a conflictual state with each other, then meet and finally merge, that their spectators discover them. In juxtaposing imagination and reality the film presents two parallel worlds which, as the story and the characters develop, will both lead towards a single outcome.

It is not a coincidence that the leads in del Toro's films are often children. The years of childhood, perhaps because they are not yet too influenced by the discontents of our civilization, are characterized by greater spontaneity and openness to unusual experiences. As a result, the boundaries between perceptions of the external world and fantasy, also reflecting those between preconscious and unconscious mental functioning, are in children less sharply defined, thus allowing for more fluidity. As the obvious precursor to films with children getting drawn into magical realms, I hardly need to mention the Hollywood classic *The Wizard of Oz* (Fleming 1938). And, as we have seen earlier in this chapter with Saura's *Cría Cuervos* and Erice's *The Spirit of the Beehive*, children with their capacity for magical thinking are present with impressive results in other Spanish-language films.

Ofelia, the protagonist of *Pan's Labyrinth,* is a prepubescent girl of about eleven years of age, a time that is on the cusp of major anatomical, physiological and psychological changes, a fact consistent with the film's historical setting and the logic of its narrative. Specifically, as del Toro explained, "her age is one when we put away our toys, we put away our fairy tales, and we put away our souls, to become just another adult. That crossroads we have all grown through. . . . The moment of loss of childhood is a profoundly melancholic one in all our lives."

In the film we are presented with an almost hyper-realistic environment, precisely located in place (Spain) and time (June 1944), and steeped in the tensions of military conflict, institutional violence, and abusive personal relationships. This is contrasted with a mythological timeless universe of fairy tales and fantasy, of magic powers and strange creatures. Several objects cathected with symbolic and almost fetishistic significance (a watch, a piece of chalk, an hourglass, a dagger, the *Book of Crossroads*, a key – not to mention the labyrinth itself with its suggestively shaped gateway) can be found to belong to both realms, or even physically to cross the borders between them, thus evoking in the film's viewers a most uncanny sensation.

Guided by a fairy, we follow our heroine Ofelia as she enters the mental labyrinth of the unique space-time of her imagination in order to avoid the humiliations, suffering and losses of her daily existence. In the process, she meets a number of fantastic characters who, in del Toro's own words, represent liberating forces, as they deal with our imperfections to which we have to become reconciled, instead of aspiring to perfection. However, Ofelia also discovers that the fantasy world itself can be as (or even more) frightening as the one she had tried to escape, populated as it is by monstrous creatures who demand total obedience from her and challenge her to almost impossible performances. This imaginary space could also function as a sort of training ground where children can learn to grow up by completing difficult tasks and overcoming traumatic experiences, or to where they could regress in the course of their private investigations into such anxiety-provoking, but also exciting, subjects as sexuality and the mystery of how babies are conceived.

"I very deliberately designed the idea of the fantasy world to be extremely uterine," del Toro explained; "we used a fallopian palette of colours: we used crimsons and golds, and everything in the fantasy world is very rounded while everything in the real world is cold and straight. You can see it in the not-so-subtle entrance to the tree. When we did the poster for the movie for Cannes, somebody said they wanted to call the movie *A Womb with a View*. The point is that this girl's idea of heaven, ultimately, is to go back into her mother's belly" (del Toro in Mark Kermode's interview, 2006). Such a place of fantasy can also be understood as one which young girls such as Ofelia create in order to be in charge of their own decisions, while in the real world they feel excluded from the powerful grownups: both those who behave sadistically like Captain Vidal, and those who act with heroism like the housemaid Mercedes and the good doctor Ferreiro.

In Ofelia we come across a constant tension, characteristic of all growing children, between obedience and rebellion to authority, whether that of the cruel step-father or of the more benign (but also demanding) faun. Del Toro described her as "a girl who needs to disobey anything except her own soul." As to Ofelia's mother, she is pathetically paralyzed in her destiny as the captain's wife, and as his child's bearer. Weak of character and physically unhealthy in her pregnant condition, Carmen is a woman defeated by her tragic life vicissitudes and therefore unable to be the good-enough parent that Ofelia so desperately needs. The girl, however, finds a second mother in the more positive figure of Mercedes, the servant who risks her life to help her own brother and his comrades, and who adopts Ofelia under her wing. We watch Mercedes hugging Ofelia, comforting her when she is afraid, and singing her a beautiful lullaby.

It may be of interest to point out here at least some of the numerous, if only implied, references that del Toro's sophisticated script and iconology make to all sorts of popular stories, characters and mythologies. Ofelia's rebellion against the faun's instructions constitutes a variation on the biblical theme of original sin: driven by her childish Pleasure Principle, she eats two grapes that look like *balls*, or *eyes*, in an act of castration reminding us of Oedipus' self-inflicted blindness. This moment is followed by the punishment which will lead to the death of the girl's mother during childbirth (the expulsion from the Garden of Eden), but also to Ofelia's chance of being offered a last-minute very Christian forgiveness for her disobedience. In that same scene the monstrous (yet still anthropomorphic) Pale Creature who catches and eats the flying fairies is inspired by Francisco Goya's so-called 'black painting' of *Saturn Devouring His Son*, while the monster placing his eyes into orbits in his hands seems to condense two disturbing images from Luis Buñuel's surrealistic masterpiece *Un Chien Andalou* (1929).

Being given a rigid deadline ("You must come back before the last grain of sand in the hourglass falls") makes us think of Cinderella having to rush home from the ball before midnight, like so many other adolescents after her. The writhing

Figure 3.4 Ivana Baquero in *Pan's Labyrinth* (del Toro 2006)

mandrake root (an unnatural crossing of borders from the vegetable to the animal kingdom) which Ofelia puts under her pregnant mother's bed to try to save her life looks almost like a quotation from Svankmajer's *Little Otik* (2000). And in Ofelia's refusal to let the faun draw blood from her baby brother, with whom she identifies as the helpless victim, there is perhaps a reference to King Solomon's decision leading to a mother's own sacrifice in order to protect a threatened child, as well as an echo of Abraham's sacrifice of his son Isaac.

I should also mention that in the classical fairy-tale trope of being given three tasks to complete in order to become a real princess (rather than to marry one, like in Turandot and in many other such stories), we find a variation on the theme of the Three Caskets, interpreted by Freud (1913a) with reference to *The Merchant of Venice* and *King Lear*. Indulging here in a bit of free association, the production design of *Pan's Labyrinth* might even make us think of *A Midsummer's Night Dream*, though del Toro's fantasy is about a much darker forest than the Shakespearean one. Last but not least, the assumption underscoring the whole film about the existence of a magical world only perceivable by those who believe in it reminds us of two classic English stories: *Alice's Adventures in Wonderland* (Carroll 1865) and *Peter Pan* (Barrie 1911). Perhaps, though, the dominant atmosphere in *Pan's Labyrinth* is more reminiscent of the one pervading Hans Christian Andersen's fairy tales.

All these and other allusions, drawn as they are from the vast body of del Toro's literary, cinematic, historical and popular culture, filtered through his artistic sensitivity, provide a backcloth to the whole texture of his film. We can suggest here an analogy with the way in which, as we learn from psychoanalytic theory, day residues are assembled and combined together in order to form the fabric of dreams. In movies like *Pan's Labyrinth* we can identify similarities between the dream work, which involves the use of such mechanisms as displacement, condensation and secondary revision, and the film work, which involves the creative selection and editing of such a rich array of building blocks and visual furniture. As we have seen in Chapter One, films are not dreams, but both share a facility for integrating within their narratives different layers of external reality and inner experiences.

I would now like to go back to a theme I had introduced earlier and suggest that *Pan's Labyrinth* succeeds precisely because it manages to remain suspended in that transitional territory where two different psychological and narrative modalities coexist in a state of creative tension. On the one hand it is clear that, as she immerses herself in the faun's underworld by letting herself be seduced into its spiral labyrinth, Ofelia (whose name cannot but remind us of Hamlet's lover gone mad with despair) also enters a psychotic, hallucinatory and delusional space-time, from which, not unlike Orpheus's wife, Eurydice, she might eventually find it impossible to emerge. But as Daniela Merigliano (2010) points out, "*Pan's Labyrinth* reminds us that the netherworld guarantees protection from the sufferings of the world of the living." This involves, in Ofelia's case, having recourse to the unconscious process of splitting from external reality whenever she is faced with the anxiety caused by the traumas and losses which life keeps presenting her. It is quite remarkable, by the way, that she does not also use the mechanism of denial, so often associated with splitting. In the presence of the faun, Ofelia seems to remain well aware of the tragic events in her life overground and makes frequent references to them. Conversely, she brings to her existence on earth the knowledge and even some of the objects (such as the magic piece of chalk) she had acquired during her time in the labyrinth.

On the other hand, del Toro's film presents us spectators with a seamless fluctuation in a girl's mind: from historical to fairy-tale realities; from, say, the military world of the captain to the earthly-rooted one of the faun; from Ofelia's existence as a desperate young girl doomed to be killed to her destiny to become an immortal princess. Such a fluctuation is represented through the coexistence of contrasting temporalities: a present of often intolerable suffering superimposed onto a nostalgic past – of heroic gestures for some, of royal bliss for others – and to a future of change and hope. Their meeting-point is symbolized by the watch deliberately frozen by the captain's father at the moment of his death. The fluidity between these spaces and these temporalities, visually mirrored in the merging of different narrative and representational styles within the film (such as its evolving use of sounds, colours and lights), provides pointers to the psychological permeability of the boundaries between the young protagonist's different states of mind.

As psychoanalysts we are well placed to have special access to our analysands' inner worlds (and, through theirs, to our own too). Their inevitable resistances notwithstanding, we are privy to many of their fantasies, their distorted childhood memories constructed in *après-coup,* their secret fears and desires and, of course, their dreams and nightmares. In our daily practice we find ourselves having to distinguish between what really happened in their lives and their unique experience of it, while at the same time knowing that, even if the two could be clearly differentiated, we would still privilege the subjective, internal version of their life events over the objective, historical one.

When offered another opportunity to immerse ourselves, away from our consulting rooms, in a space-time where disparately experienced realities collide, intersect or merge, and when we are therefore given a fresh view of the world from the magic bridges stretched across them (as is the case when watching films like *Pan's Labyrinth*), even we psychoanalysts cannot but gasp with surprise and wonderment.[9]

*****

Del Toro's film has shown us, among other things, the dramatic consequences of military conflict on a young girl, as well as the remarkable resources available to her through her fantasy life in an effort to survive in a hostile world. The theme of how wars in the first half of the twentieth century have profoundly upset, when not altogether destroyed, the hopes and lives of so many children all over Europe had also been treated with the starkest of realism by Roberto Rossellini.

Together with film directors Luchino Visconti and Vittorio De Sica, Rossellini is the main exponent of Italian *Neorealismo*. This term refers to a new approach to filmmaking that emerged in the 1940s from the individually and collectively traumatizing experiences of Fascism, the Second World War and the Resistance. Often filming on location with natural lights, nonprofessional actors and minimal use of props, yet at the same time experimenting with new forms of camera work and editing techniques, these filmmakers deliberately attempted to reproduce a culturally unmediated reality, documenting in the process some of its socially and historically most disturbing aspects. This neorealistic tendency was to last only a few years but was to indirectly influence cinema to the present day. It is in marked contrast with, say, the Expressionistic movement of the previous decades, which was especially prominent in German cinema, and which makes florid use of symbolism and emphasizes anything that calls attention to the film as artifice.

Following *Rome, Open City* (1945) and *Paisà* (1946), *Germany Year Zero* (1948)[10] is the last in Rossellini's so-called *Trilogia della Guerra (Trilogy of War)* (see Rossellini, Roncoronis, and Amidei 1973) and the first of his works made abroad. He drove alone to Germany in March 1947, apparently still without any particular story in mind, partly in order to internationalize the subject of war, which had recently made him famous with his two previous works, and partly to look for an answer to his own troubling question: "The Germans were human beings like everybody else. What could have led them to this disaster?" (Rossellini 1973). He found a story to tell but, needless to say, no answer to his question.

Rossellini's film is an unsentimental documentation of the social and economic consequences of large-scale manmade tragedies. Watching this film one can hardly imagine how a country (Germany in this case, but it may equally be

Vietnam or Kosovo or Syria) could ever recover from the conditions into which the horrors of destruction and genocide have plunged it. At a different level, *Germany Year Zero* is characterized by a pessimistic sense of individual existential despair. Its story is the chronicle of a few days in the life of twelve-year-old Edmund Koehler (Edmund Meschke) and his family, struggling to survive in the misery of postwar Berlin. Two of the film's characters, devastated like post-Nazi Germany itself by shame and guilt, state several times: "I wish I were dead." A third one acts that wish out: Edmund will kill his own father before jumping from the ruins of a building to his own death. This hopelessness must also be considered in the context of Rossellini's own personal tragedy, the film being dedicated to the memory of his recently deceased first child, the eight-year-old boy Romano.

While sharing a markedly neorealistic approach, as well as the main subject, with the two other films in the trilogy, *Germany Year Zero* (as a critic has convincingly argued in his monograph on Rossellini) also contains numerous elements belonging to what he calls "dark Expressionism" (Brunette 1987, p. 82). This is evident, for instance, in the symbolism of a cityscape of rubble, allegorically portraying the disintegration of values of its inhabitants; in the deliberate focusing of Rossellini's camera, during a crucial scene, on an anonymous child holding the hand of an old man almost to represent the continuity of history; in the stylized use of very contrasted black-and-white photography that emphasizes the conflict between moral darkness and light, between evil and good; or, finally, in the clash between the exteriors shot on location in Berlin and the artificially claustrophobic interiors shot in a Roman studio:[11] a formally complex film behind a simple narrative structure and stark visual appearance.

After a long, dramatic running shot through what is left of the city of Berlin as background to the opening credits, *Germany Year Zero* zooms on twelve-year-old Edmund scrapping a living for his family by gravedigging and picking up bits of coal fallen on the pavement (there is a similar scene in Frank McCourt's memoir *Angela's Ashes* 1996), while passers-by carve out a miserable piece of meat from a horse collapsed in the street. Surviving involves the use of adjustment techniques, similar to those described by sociologist Erving Goffman (1961) in relation to "total institutions," in a world dominated, in this case, not by authoritarian order but by its opposite: chaos and lack of boundaries. The frantic and relentless tempo of Rossellini's concise film (it only lasts 78 minutes), with everyone rushing almost all the time in a city where there is nothing else to do than to keep alive, conveys to the viewers the overwhelming inner anxiety and sense of personal and social devastation that pervades just about everything occurring on the screen.

Berlin, the bleak real protagonist of the film,[12] is here both the former capital of the Third Reich, a precise historical and geographical *topos,* and a universal symbol standing for any place at any time (Troy, Hiroshima, Baghdad) where war has left behind destruction and suffering. The scenario looks surreal, with barren landscapes of bomb sites located somewhere between Giovan Battista

Figure 3.5 Germany Year Zero (Rossellini 1948)

Piranesi's etchings of Rome and Giorgio de Chirico's eerie paintings of meta-physical squares.

In such a city the clothes on still-warm corpses are considered for their value on the marketplace. A gramophone record of the Führer's inflammatory speeches (consisting, ironically, of a crass attempt to deny history) can be sold to the occupy-ing soldiers as a tourist souvenir. Hospitals are buildings where one goes for a free meal. Children's labour, and their bodies, are commodities to be taken advantage of. The remains of the chancellery are treated as if they were an archaeological site, the background for a photograph to be sent back home to one's girlfriend. Depriva-tion, poverty, hunger and exhaustion, in a society furthermore humiliated by defeat, Rossellini seems to tell us, are no breeding ground for the political solidarity or Christian charity which characterize some of his other films. What flourish instead are widespread corruption, black marketeering, theft, lies, hypocrisy and abuse.

Such all-pervasiveness of violence culminates in Edmund's double killing. These are the desperate gestures of a child still under the Nazi ideological pres-sure from the previous generation, represented here by his former schoolteacher. "The weak perish, the strong survive. That's nature," Herr Enning asserts, poi-sonously perverting a Darwinian principle. Edmund can only (mis)understand it as an encouragement to murder his own sick father, which he does by poisoning him – using, that is, the same weapon that, in *Cría Cuervos,* Ana had mistakenly believed had killed her own father. In Edmund's disturbed mind such an act was a form of euthanasia to help his family survive by sacrificing its most vulner-able member – until he realizes the enormity of it and is then overwhelmed by suicidal guilt.

Let us briefly consider these dramatic events in *Germany Year Zero* in the more specific context of a child's experience of traumatic losses. Everyone, in the year zero of European history, had lost something precious: a relative, a limb, dignity, a home, a friend, income, social identity. *Spes, ultima dea*: hope, in a hopelessly devastated world, remains the last goddess to die when all, villains and heroes alike, are still trying to hold on, tooth-and-nail, to whatever little they have.

A tragic consequence of such losses from the perspective of children is that they find themselves forced by circumstances to behave like adults. It is not a coincidence that the first dialogue in the film is a discussion about Edmund's age. Still a young boy, we know that he has already lost his mother, as well as having been exposed to the cumulative effects of the multiple traumatization of having lived his short life under a dictatorship, and half of it in a state of war. To survive he has to relinquish his childhood and prematurely become, and not just pretend to be, a man: to face responsibilities which he can hardly be expected to fulfill, such as looking financially and emotionally after his family; but also, in the most extreme form, to commit such "adult" acts as homicide and suicide.

These acts, I suggest, are the expression of his unconscious rebellion against his elders' abusive behaviour against him, and against children in general. I am not only referring here to Herr Enning's shameless paedophilic exploitation, nor to the viciously aggressive and dishonest behaviour of Herr Rademaker, the family's landlord. I am also thinking of Edmund's father himself, who in an emotionally poignant scene feels justified in slapping his child on the face ("Come here . . . nearer . . .") as punishment for not returning home the previous night – something which the boy could not have helped anyway. Physical abuse of this kind is presented here as the normal way in which parents discipline their children. But then we should remember that Herr Koehler, an otherwise more benign character than most others in the film, is himself the product of a culture whose values were rooted in those same authoritarian educational principles that, as we know, had played a key role in producing the Nazi generation. These were principles according to which children are objects whose personality must be moulded by any available means for the purpose of perpetuating a rigidly hierarchical social order. "The authoritarian state," writes Wilhelm Reich, "has a representative in every family, the father; in this way he becomes the state's most valuable tool. [He] produces submissiveness to authority in his children, especially his sons. This is the basis of the passive, submissive attitude of middle class individuals towards Führer figures" (Reich 1933, p. 45).

"Every film I make," Rossellini told Mario Verdone in 1952, "interests me for a particular scene, perhaps for a finale I already have in mind. . . . *Germany Year Zero*, to tell the truth, was conceived specifically for the scene with the child wandering on his own through the ruins." In the film's powerful, nearly wordless concluding sequences, we see Edmund walking aimlessly through what is left of his city and being let down by everyone who could instead have been on his side.

Then Edmund stops and, almost without thinking about it, he finds himself playing a solitary game of hopscotch. For a brief, magic moment squashed between parricide and suicide we can allow ourselves a smile, as Edmund lets himself at long last regress to being a child again.

Notes

1. Hollywood's contribution to this genre is vast. It includes classics such as *The Wizard of Oz* (Fleming 1938) with Judy Garland, the cute performances of young stars such as little princess Shirley Temple or Macaulay Culkin left home alone, and the large number of films (often of dubious quality) in the coming-of-age category. Leaving those aside, some of my many favourite classics are the following: Ozu's *Record of a Tenement's Gentleman* (1947) about a lost boy who, left with a widow, struggles to convince her to look after him; Buñuel's *Los Olvidados* (1950) on the tragedy of the forgotten children of Mexico City's poor neighborhoods; Visconti's *Bellissima* (1951) on a mother's obsession with her little girl getting a part in a film; Truffaut's *The 400 Blows* (1959) on the semi-autobiographical vicissitudes of a neglected boy turning to petty crime; Tornatore's *Cinema Paradiso* (1988) about a child's lifelong passion for cinema; Doillon's *Ponette* (1996) on a four-year old girl coming to terms with the death of her mother; Sveràk's *Kolya* (1996) about a cellist growing attached to a five-year-old boy left to him against his wishes; Salles's *Central Station* (1998) about a boy travelling across Brazil with an older woman in search of his father; and the Dardenne brothers' *The Kid with a Bike* (2011) on the relationship between a difficult child and the town hairdresser who fosters him on weekends.
2. *Kes* (Great Britain 1969). Directed by Ken Loach. Writers Ken Loach, Tony Garnett and Barry Hines from his novel *A Kestrel for a Knave*. Starring David Bradley (Billy Casper), Brian Glover ("Bobby Charlton"), and Colin Welland (Mr Farthing).
3. Colin Welland, the actor who played Mr Farthing, stated in an interview: "The great thing about *Kes* was that it was warts-and-all and the kids still love it. I didn't act in it. It was just me being me and it's one of the best things I've ever done."
4. *The Spirit of the Beehive [El espíritu de la colmena]* (Spain 1973). Directed and written by Victor Erice. Starring Fernando Fernán Gómez (Fernando), Teresa Gimpera (Teresa), Ana Torrent (Ana), and Isabel Tellería (Isabel).
5. *Cría Cuervos* (Spain 1976). Directed and written by Carlos Saura. Starring Héctor Alterio (Anselmo), Geraldine Chaplin (Maria and Ana as a young woman), Conchita Pérez (Irene), Ana Torrent (Ana), Maite Sánchez (Maite), and Josefina Díaz (grandmother).
6. The film's title comes from a chilling Spanish saying: *Cría cuervos y te sacarán los ojos (Raise ravens and they'll pluck your eyes)*.
7. *Pan's Labyrinth [El laberinto del fauno]* (Spain and Mexico 2006). Directed and written by Guillermo del Toro. Starring Ivana Baquero (Ofelia) and Sergi Lòpez (Captain Vidal).
8. *Pan's Labyrinth* was nominated for six Oscars (of which it won three) and received countless other international awards. Critics described it as "a magical motion picture" (Berardinelli, 2007) and as "one of the greatest of all fantasy films . . . visually stunning" (Ebert 2007).
9. I have explored these issues in more detail in *Boundaries and Bridges: Perspectives on Time and Space in Psychoanalysis*, Sabbadini 2014.
10. *Germany Year Zero [Germania anno zero]* (Italy 1948). Directed and written by Roberto Rossellini. Starring Edmund Meschke (Edmund Koehler) and Ernst Pittschau (the father).

11. There is an amusing story about it: apparently, during the month they spent in Rome, the starving cast of German semiprofessional actors put on considerable weight by eating tons of *pastasciutta*. "The pieces didn't go together on the editing table," reported Rossellini, "because the tall and thin gentleman walking the streets of Berlin, and approaching a door, when the door was opened, was another person, well fed and with the face of well-being." Apparently, filming had to be suspended for two weeks during which time the actors went on a diet (Faldini and Fofi 1979).

12. Even bleaker than another urban postwar protagonist of a masterpiece of those years, the Vienna of *The Third Man* (Carol Reed 1949).

...and slightly older ones
Films on adolescents

As already noted in the previous chapter, psychoanalysis is primarily a developmental psychology, that is a theory of the human mind that attributes fundamental importance to past events (both external and internal) for the understanding of present ones. Even if in contemporary psychoanalysis the emphasis in clinical work has moved away from reconstructions of the past to a more central role for the here-and-now experience of transference and countertransference, there is no doubt that the developmental dimension has remained paramount. This still leaves much room for a variety of theories about the nature and timing of such development. Some authors, for instance, emphasize a series of stages (Freud, Erikson, Mahler), specific developmental lines (Anna Freud), or different psychological positions and the oscillations between them (Klein, Bion, Ogden).

In classical psychoanalytic views the theoretical and clinical lens has always been focused almost entirely on early childhood, with adolescence being seen as a mere regression to, or recapitulation of, earlier psychological features (such as pre-Oedipal and Oedipal fantasies, attachments and conflicts). An exception to this approach was Erik Erikson's important work on the "crisis" of adolescents trying to establish a sense of identity for themselves (Erikson 1959).

It is only in the course of the last thirty or so years that a radical shift has taken place in relation to our understanding of adolescence, when psychoanalytic authors have started to consider it as a developmental stage in its own right, with its peculiar characteristics, in both normality and psychopathology. This has had vast repercussions not only for our understanding of the adolescents' world and their problems (identity crises, eating disorders, sexual confusion and a tendency towards addictive, self-harming and suicidal behaviour), but also for our understanding of adult psychology.

In fact, in his third essay on the theory of sexuality, "The transformations of puberty," Freud (1905) had already opened the way to a reassessment of the specificity of adolescence in human development by suggesting that, although young people experience anxieties and conflicts similar to those in their own childhood, nevertheless such experiences have to take into account the all-important fact that they occur in a new, transformed body where, Freud writes, "the sexual instinct is now subordinated to the reproductive function" (Freud 1905, p. 207). The physical changes to the boy's and girl's bodies during puberty are no marginal phenomenon for our psychology, because what was for the Oedipal child an unconscious fantasy has now become for the adolescent a conscious one, that is a potential reality to be negotiated, defended against, or acted upon. As Moses and Eglé Laufer point out, "[T]he period of adolescence has a specific and essential contribution to make to psychological life and the psychic disruptions of this period need to be understood differently from those of childhood and adulthood. This difference rests on the fact that adolescence begins with physical sexual maturity" (Laufer and Laufer 1984, p. ix). These authors believe that all "manifest disruptions in behaviour and functioning during adolescence are preceded by a developmental breakdown at puberty . . . a breakdown in the process of integrating the physically mature body image into the representation of oneself" (Laufer and Laufer 1984, pp. 21–22).

What strikes us about adolescents is their constant search (sometimes exciting, other times tragic) for positive models of identification. Those working with them will be impressed by such features as (a) their curiosity about their own internal world and the external one surrounding them, leading them to all sorts of experimentations – creative at times, other times destructive; (b) their capacity for extremes of idealization and denigration; (c) their fears of losing control over their own impulses, leading to dangerous explosions of aggressiveness, sometimes directed against others (e.g. through delinquent behaviour), more often turned against the self (e.g. through drug addiction or self-mutilation); and (d) last but not least, their need for clear rules which they can respect (though they will often try and break them). This last category includes their attempts to establish safe boundaries with anyone in a position of authority, to negotiate the right amount of closeness or distance from their parents, and to allow for moving independently away from them into adulthood, that is, for separating and individuating while remaining emotionally attached to them.

Young people often fall under the attraction of two intrinsically unrealizable, yet universal, fantasies, both with rich literary and philosophical traditions: a past Golden Age and a future Utopia. The Golden Age myth refers to a time when life was bliss, and happiness was the only known human condition. ("Golden Age" is the literal translation of the *Aurea Ætas* of Ovid's *Metamorphosis*, a masterpiece of Latin poetry written two thousand years ago, though the idea of a lost Eden has existed since at least biblical times.) This fantasy is consistent with the regressive one of an innocent, joyful childhood (Jean-Jacques Rousseau's *bon sauvage*), of an all-satisfied relationship of the baby at the breast of milk-and-honey, or even of an entirely undisturbed intrauterine experience.

The second of these powerful fantasies to be frequently found among adolescents, and complementary to the first, concerns Utopia. This word, meaning literally a "no-place," that is, an island outside time and space, was first used in 1516 in the title of Sir Thomas More's essay where he describes an ideal place with a perfect social and political system. The concept of Utopia was then extended to include any ambitiously visionary program, such as those which grip the imagination of many adolescents.

Golden Age and Utopia operate according to the same Primary Process logic that dominates unconscious functioning. Furthermore, they are in many respects identical, in that their common ultimate purpose is to defend our frail egos from unacceptable realities. They both represent an escape from the truth through the psychological mechanisms of splitting the bad from the good, denying the presence of the former and projecting the latter onto places and times which, existing only in the mind, easily assume mythical proportions. In other words, by hiding away in the Golden Age and in Utopia, we manically avoid the psychic suffering of loss and mourning that should eventually be confronted if we are to come to terms with our existence without deceiving ourselves or going mad.

The problems start when such juvenile wishful fantasies clash with our own adult values, rationality or experience, and we then respond by crushing them. During adolescence it is a normal experience to allow oneself to get carried away by passionate enthusiasms for some aspects or other of existence, such as an intimate relationship, a political ideal, a social mission or any other such grandiose future plan. Adults, who tend to lose the capacity for such intense experiences, can sometimes become envious of those in the next generation who still possess it. Of course young people are often naive or misguided ("*Si jeunesse savait . . .*" say the French, "*If only young people knew . . .*") and our attempts to protect them, and ourselves, from inevitable disappointments or even catastrophic mistakes may be the best-intentioned in the world. But when we do not allow our adolescents to enjoy their passions, foolish as they may appear to us, and we do not let them learn about life and its countless complications in their own way, we should know that, in their eyes, we become insensitive and cruel – and we risk getting punished for it. While trying to limit the damage that the most extreme passions may cause young people if left unchecked, we should be grateful to them for dreaming of a better (if also unattainable) world, for there could be little realizable progress if we were left without unrealizable ideals to pursue. If we never allowed our minds to indulge in such individual or collective flights of fancy our lives would be empty and civilization itself would not exist.

*****

The theme of children driven by despair to murder and death, which we have seen so realistically represented in Rossellini's film, was also approached in an entirely different context by film director Peter Jackson. The protagonists of his *Heavenly Creatures*[1] are two adolescent girls, Pauline (Melanie Lynskey) and Juliet (Kate Winslet): when not immersed in their fantasy world, like Ana and Isabel were in *The Spirit of the Beehive* and Ofelia was in *Pan's Labyrinth*, they become obsessed with the plan to murder the mother of one of them, seen as the cause of all their unhappiness.

I would like to suggest that the real-life events which took place in Christchurch, New Zealand, in 1954 and which have become the subject of Peter Jackson's film, could be understood as a powerful illustration of the dangers of interfering with what adolescents feel passionately about: in this case the

Figure 4.1 Kate Winslet and Melanie Lynskey in *Heavenly Creatures* (Jackson 1994)

friendship between two fourteen-year-old schoolgirls and the shared fantasy on which such friendship is based ("a perversion of true love or its purest manifestation," as Adam Mars-Jones pondered on the pages of *The Independent*).

This fantasy "Fourth World," as the girls call it, reminiscent of the one described in the children's novel *The Secret Garden* (Burnett 1911) and mixed in the film with the real one through a creative use of editing and special effects, is in their words "a sort of heaven, only better, because there aren't any questions. An absolute paradise of music, art and pure enjoyment." It is paradoxical that these girls' way to eventually bring their heaven down to earth is by dreaming to escape, of all places, to Tinsel City – the place where New Zealander director Peter Jackson, a former master of horror movies with such titles in his filmography as *Bad Taste* (1987) and *Braindead* (1992), will soon after emigrate and where he will find fame with his colossally fantastic Tolkien project.

Based on the diaries written by Pauline Parker (one of the two main characters), *Heavenly Creatures* focuses on the strong, obsessive relationship, not without homosexual overtones, which Pauline (also answering to the names of Paul, Yvonne, Gina and Charles) and Juliet[2] (also called Debórah) develop with one another. When Pauline's mother tries to put an end to it, the two girls conspire to murder her, and then succeed.

A precursor of such movies on dysfunctional families as Solondz's *Happiness* (1998), Vinterberg's *Festen* (1998) and Mendes's *American Beauty* (1999), *Heavenly Creatures* was made in between its director's gory film projects and his trilogy of blockbusters (*Lord of the Rings* 2001–2003), and it borrows from both. Pauline and Juliet access their delusional world by "a gateway through the clouds." Their pie-in-the-sky contains idealized gods such as, in those pre-Elvis days, the Saint George-like tenor Mario Lanza, while lurking in the dark are the shadows of such hated devils as the Orson Welles of *The Third Man*. These references, be they to literature, music, or cinema, are themselves significant of the adolescents' need to anchor their worldview to a cultural ground which, incidentally, makes them vulnerable, more so perhaps in our days than back in the 1950s, to all sorts of commercial exploitation.

The fact that we may or may not share with our boys and girls their choice of partners, their political values, their heroes and their villains, or their taste in music and fashion, is mostly irrelevant. What matters instead is that we should not try to prevent them from finding out for themselves. Getting into conflict with adolescents over such matters, inevitable as it may at times be, is likely to increase anxieties, guilt and confusion in everyone concerned. But should such generational conflicts be avoided at all costs? Probably not. The problem, rather, is that when parents have reasons to disapprove of the behaviour of the adolescents they care for, they are faced with a central dilemma: if they intervene they interfere, if they do not intervene they are being neglectful. Either approach, motivated by the parents' past experiences and unresolved conflicts with their own parents, is likely to make young people even more alienated from those in a position of authority.

An attitude of tolerance is then necessary to at least create some space for constructive dialogue. If this collapses, as it does in *Heavenly Creatures,* the consequences can only be tragic. In the film, Pauline (oedipally) hates her mother (and loves instead her best friend's father), while Juliet tries unsuccessfully to identify with her own mother but, despite her efforts, including massive somatizations, to get her affection she still keeps being rejected and abandoned. Increasingly isolated from their parents, and mocked as "Laurel and Hardy," the two girls decide they will sink or swim together. As we already find out from the opening sequence, sink they will (even though Kate Winslet is in this film journeying on an altogether safer ocean-liner than the *Titanic* which, a few years after her performance as Juliet, will turn her into an international star).

Often, though, even an understanding attitude, especially if it feels hypocritical because it is not backed up by the provision of positive models of identification, is not sufficient. Parents and other assorted experts have in Jackson's film opportunities to make fools of themselves by uttering grand pseudo-psychological statements about unhealthy friendships, unwholesome attachments and "passing phases" of homosexuality (that nasty condition which one day, we are told, science will undoubtedly eradicate). Not to mention Juliet's mother, a marriage guidance counselor herself, who uses her special brand of "deep therapy" to seduce one of her patients into a most unhealthy, unwholesome *ménage à trois* perfectly complementing her daughter's alleged *folie à deux*.

It must be said, though, that even those adults who are better qualified to deal with adolescents, such as good-enough parents, find themselves faced again and again with impossible decisions which may have crucial consequences for their relationship with their children. Often their dilemma consists, as suggested above, of turning a blind eye and letting something be in order not to magnify a problem that would have soon gone away on its own (or, indeed, in order to avoid creating one that did not exist in the first place), which may well be the wisest thing to do. Or is the wiser solution, on the other hand, to face the issue openly and deal with it before it is too late? In *Heavenly Creatures* we see adolescents and their parents struggling with such family dramas. If, in the end, our sympathies can oscillate between the generations and we are left trying to understand instead of trying to blame, this can only be evidence of the maturity of Peter Jackson's film.

*****

Children and adolescents can find themselves entrapped in violence by the social circumstances in which they happen to live. Slums around the world are not only places of great misery and physical suffering, but also breeding grounds of abuse and violence. A good example of this are the Brazilian *favelas.*

A work of fiction, yet based on actual events that occurred in Rio de Janeiro in the 1960s and 1970s (where things have only been improving in the last few years), Fernando Meirelles's *City of God*[3] is a devastatingly powerful portrait of the social and moral reality of Brazilian *favelas* (and things are probably not much different elsewhere). Such a condition, the film implies, is tolerated, if not actively encouraged, by governments incompetent or unwilling to deal with the problems – extreme poverty and social injustice – that feed its existence.

All societies tend to marginalize those of their members whose behaviour, or even just whose presence, they find unacceptable. These unacceptable people are placed into literally and metaphorically separate areas: the schizophrenic in the lunatic asylum, the whore in the red-light district, the criminal in the prison, the corpse buried in the graveyard, the hoodlum rampaging in the shanty-town. . . . Sometimes they are kept at a safe distance from the civilized world of those who consider themselves to be normal, other times just next door to it (*favelas* often border wealthy neighbourhoods). It seems that for those fortunate enough to belong elsewhere, these locations can also function as targets of massive projections. In people's fantasies these places thus become the receptacles of much more than is actually there: more sadistic attacks, more hallucinogenic drug abuse, wilder frenzied madness, more transgressive polymorphous perversities. At times, however, things are actually even more extreme than we may imagine them to be. For instance, those of us who before watching *City of God* were unfamiliar with the reality of Brazilian slums may not have been aware of the role played in them by young children. In this respect, the film must also be valued as an important document about this tragic social phenomenon.

City of God is one of the key films in the recent *Buena Onda* (Good Wave) renaissance of Latin American cinema. It makes a compelling use of an original narrative style, of a large cast of local, carefully selected and well trained nonprofessional actors, and of such techniques as breakneck-speed cutting in the editing, shooting with hand-held cameras, using color-coded filters to signify different periods of time, split screens, speeded-up action sequences, and repeated scenes sometimes shot from a slightly different point of view as a device to introduce new details. Compared by some critics to Martin Scorsese's *Goodfellas* (1990),

City of God is, in the words of one of them, "part tender coming-of-age film and part gang-warfare epic from the Brazilian *favela* told from the viewpoint of the children who manage to be both its underclass and its criminal overlords. The City of God is like one vast, dysfunctional family, neighbours from hell with no neighbours, with no parents or concerned adults. It is a cross between an orphanage and an abattoir" (Bradshaw 2003). A gun culture, then, that does not spare young kids as both its victims and perpetrators; a violence that is pervasive, as well as often gratuitous; corruption contaminating the very police force that should instead fight against it; the massive spread of drug dealing and drug addiction; the lack of family and community support, as well as of positive models of identification. These are the realities dominating the existence of *favela* dwellers, cornered into the *Cidade de Deus* that gives its ironic title to the film.

Much as they try, most of those born in it cannot get out. I am reminded here, *mutatis mutandis*, of Luis Buñuel's film *The Exterminating Angel* (1962) where, after a dinner party, the guests are unable, in that case for rather surrealistic reasons, to leave their hosts' mansion. The *favela*'s dwellers are born inside a trap and in that same trap they are doomed to die, most likely at a young age. Such a sense of entrapment is an experience some of us know about from our psychoanalytic work with patients who as children were raised within physically, emotionally and sexually abusive families or institutions. The almost insurmountable obstacles they find in stepping out from such conditions are often painfully reexperienced by these patients in the transference and by ourselves in the countertransference, as our therapeutic understanding and skills can become almost paralyzed.

While *City of God* should be seen as expressing quite literally the dehumanizing realities and resulting collective and individual suffering of a section of contemporary Brazilian society, it can also be interpreted as representing a wider human condition affecting all those who find themselves unable, for whatever complex reasons, to overcome the hurdles that life puts between them and the achievement of their ambitions or the realization of their dreams.

In the *favela*, becoming an adult, and indeed survival itself, are equated from early childhood with owning a gun rather than, say, with learning to read and write: "Are you crazy? You're just a kid!" "A kid? I smoke, snort, I've killed and robbed. I'm a man," boasts a child no more than ten or twelve years old.

Honest work is hardly an option in an environment dominated by the greedy making, and losing, of a fast *Real*. Gang culture, where the respect for leaders is based on fear rather than loyalty, is a poor relation to family and community solidarity. Only the naïve can expect kindness and compassion to thrive where ruthlessness and revenge are the accepted values.

Yet a young man known as Rocket (Alexander Rodrigues), one of the *favela*'s adolescent dwellers and the narrator of *City of God* – not unlike, self-referentially, both film director Fernando Meirelles and Paulo Lins, the author of the novel on which the movie is based – seems to succeed in somehow escaping its deadly entrapment. Through a mixture of diplomatic skills, human decency (which can occasionally be helpful even in a slum) and the sheer good luck of finding himself

Figure 4.2 City of God (Meirelles 2002)

in the right place at the right time, Rocket, while flirting with crime, also develops a secret passion for photography. As he gets behind a camera, from victim of the slum he immediately becomes its recorder, the witness and the reporter of its tragically repetitive history. The fact that his camera is a stolen one seems to suggest that Rocket knows how to use creatively, rather than dishonestly, an object belonging to a culture of criminality. Antagonist to Rocket and indeed to everyone else, the antihero of the film is the heartless gang-leader Li'l Zé (Leandro Firmino), who appears to be as emotionally blind as Rocket is instead visually alert. We watch Li'l Zé grow up into an ambition-driven and power-hungry young man who seems unstoppable, other than by bullets, in his attempts to rule the *favela*.

I would now like to refer to a couple of the most dramatic scenes in *City of God* involving Li'l Zé which seem to provide explicit illustrations of two central and interrelated mythologies described by Freud in his reconstructions of human history, both personal and collective.

In the first of these sequences Li'l Zé figuratively "castrates" two of the *favela*'s children by shooting them in the foot when he experiences the boys as potential threats to his figuratively paternal authority. The implicit reference here is to the Sophoclean tragedy of *Oedipus, King of Thebes*, which begins with the intended filicide of Oedipus, still a baby then, on the grounds that he was predicted to be threatening the authority of Laius, father and king. Jocasta, Oedipus' mother and then wife, tells the story:

> *And my son – God's mercy! – scarcely the third day was gone,*
> *When Laius took, and by another's hand*
> *Out on the desert mountain, where the land*
> *Is rock, cast him to die. Through both his feet*
> *A blade of iron they drove. Thus did we cheat*

Apollo of his will. My child could slay
No father, and the King could cast away
The fear that dogged him, by his child to die
Murdered

Sophocles, *Oedipus, King of Thebes*, pp. 183–184

The Oedipal child in the psychoanalytic version of the Greek tragedy, guilty for his sexual longings towards his mother and aggressive fantasies against his father, fears the punishment of castration. Such a castration anxiety is also an unconscious condensation of Oedipus' damaged feet, and his self-inflicted blindness after the discovery of his own patricidal and incestuous crimes.

The other scene I want to mention here is the one where the Runts, a new generation of hoodlums-in-the-bud armed by their "fathers" but ultimately disloyal to them, gang up to rebel against Li'l Zé until, at the end of the film, they shoot him dead. Li'l Zé is killed not by another gang leader such as his arch-rival Carrot, nor by a police force too corrupt to be effective, but by prepubescent children who take turns in casually unloading their guns in his back. In the godless *City of God* it is cruel revenge, when it is not mindless and meaningless violence, that dictates its bleak history. What is tragic here is not so much Li'l Zé's death (he was the villain of the piece, after all), but his killers' complete unawareness (they are only kids) that with their actions they also reassert their own entrapped condition. By killing the "father" whom they idealize and with whom they identify, they actually become like him, thus condemning themselves to become the future fathers of other patricidal sons. The cycle of violence is reenacted ad infinitum. Repetition compulsion runs across the generations. The kids are doomed.

This scene illustrates the other Freudian myth, Oedipal again in its structure and the almost inevitable consequence of the first one, concerning the children's jealousy of, and hostility against, the original father. Eventually, the jealous children take their revenge by ganging up to massacre him (and, in the totemic meal version of it, also to eat his body) in order to acquire his power and his women. In the fourth essay of *Totem and Taboo* Freud states: "The violent primal father had doubtless been the feared and envied model of each one of the company of brothers; and in the act of devouring him they accomplished their identification with him, and each one of them acquired a portion of his strength" (Freud 1913b, p. 142).

Implied in these mythological, sociohistorical, filmic or psychoanalytic narratives is, of course, the vast theme of sexuality. Even if only marginally addressed in *City of God*, its underlying importance in shaping its characters, their relationships and their vicissitudes is ever-present. In particular, Li'l Zé's clumsiness with women must account for at least some of his sadistic cruelty; it is a reflection of his emotional blindness, insensitivity and incapacity to identify with others, if not also of his actual physical impotence outside the context of rape. I am suggesting here that his psychopathic need to assert power through abuse, violence and murder against men is also an attempt to compensate for his lack of potency in relation to women. Closely associated to these dynamics is his, and other characters', envy towards those like Benny and Rocket who aspire, and to some extent succeed, to form rewarding, stable and mutually respectful object relationships based on love rather than on hatred.

Another related manifestation of what I have described as Li'l Zé's emotional blindness is his overblown narcissism. It emerges in particular as he gloats with childish exhibitionistic satisfaction when he finds the self-aggrandizing picture of himself, surrounded by fellow hoodlums and big phallic weapons, on the front page of the *Jornal do Brasil*. His narcissistic sense of omnipotence prevents him from conscious realization that the image that confers upon him a short-lived popularity among his fellow gangsters and the newspaper's voyeuristic readers is also going to be his death sentence. Unable to get in touch with his own unconscious guilt driving him towards self-destruction, Li'l Zé ends up enacting it. What finally provides him with some access, however spurious, to the world outside the *favela* turns out to be his downfall. Paradoxically, that same photograph that precipitates Li'l Zé's damnation represents for Rocket a potential bridge away from the sufferings of the *favela* and towards the world outside. For Rocket it is a step which we, the film viewers, perhaps over-optimistically, would like to believe will lead towards his salvation.

*****

Bulgarian cinema may still be little-known to Western audiences, but like its more developed and better distributed Romanian neighbour it is producing some extremely interesting works. One of them to be relevant to our exploration of themes related to adolescence is *Mila from Mars*.[4] While, as we have seen, most of the youngsters inhabiting the *City of God* remained entrapped inside it with dire consequences, Mila, thanks to her own psychological resources and the solidarity of a most unlikely group of elderly peasants, will find a way to emerge from her assorted predicaments.

The eponymous protagonist of *Mila from Mars* is a disturbed sixteen-year-old girl who, as we learn from the first shots of the movie, has been for some time a victim of physical abuse. On centre stage for most of the film, Mila (Vasela Kazakova) displays considerable cunning and determination in running away from her unscrupulous sociopathic boyfriend and pimp Alex. The powerful impact that her presence has on the viewers, however, is in contrast with the obvious precariousness of her condition, highlighted by film director and screenwriter Zornitsa Sophia through a number of technical devices. For instance, the many images shot at a tilted thirty-degree angle suggest perceptive and emotional disturbance, while the use of several jump-cuts in the editing indicates a sense of fragmentation of thought processes. Flashbacks, some of them lasting only a fraction of a second, reproduce in the audience the flashback experiences in the character's own memory – something we know to be a common phenomenon also in the posttraumatic stress disorder from which Mila is likely to suffer, given what we know about her past and what we can infer from some of her current disturbed behaviour.

Literally and metaphorically standing on her thin, anorexic long legs, almost as if she were one of Alberto Giacometti's sculptures, Mila's main feature is her vulnerability, a condition further increased by her being pregnant. When the chronological inter-titles make us viewers aware of her condition, this has the effect of inducing in at least some of us, myself included, a sense of parental protection, a sentiment also reflected in the attitude towards her of the elderly village inhabitants. Younger spectators, I guess, would instead identify with Mila herself and her predicament as a single mother-to-be.

The images from the early part of the film that remain most vividly in the mind are the long shots and mid-shots, and finally close-ups, of Mila sitting on the steps of a dilapidated building while the villagers stare at her with a mixture of puzzlement and compassion, wondering to one another about who this strange-looking girl could be (an alien from Mars, maybe?) and what they could do to rescue her from her rather miserable condition. Eventually they welcome Mila and offer her their "kindness of strangers," in spite of her adolescent sulky silences, her reluctance to express the gratitude they well deserve, and her generally passive-aggressive attitude towards them.

As they witness and comment on the events, but also act upon them, their function is comparable to that of the chorus in Greek tragedies. And it is a tragicomic twist to the story that, through their cannabis growing and smuggling activities, these old folk should themselves have become the unlikely victims of exploitation by that same devilish Alex who had been taking advantage of Mila.

We can also presume that their psychological reasons to intervene may not be entirely selfless, for they must have attributed to this young and attractive newcomer, landed from nowhere on their doorsteps, all sorts of qualities they had themselves lost many years earlier and which they could secretly hope to recover by relating to her.

For most of the film we see Mila withdrawn into silence and in a state of regression. Presumably suffering from the emotional consequences of never

Figure 4.3 Vasela Kazakova in *Mila from Mars* (Sophia 2004)

fully mourned early losses (of parents, of innocence, of trust in others, of self-confidence), not to mention more recent traumatizations, she is not just running away from her current intolerable situation but is also actively searching for a safe place where she might somehow come to terms with her painful past. I consider it significant that Mila should be left nameless for most of the film, letting herself utter her own name for the first time only near the end, when she begins to emerge from her isolation – no longer, perhaps, someone from Mars – and to exist as a real person.

As already suggested, Mila's need to escape from abuse and to regress into a protected space is reinforced by her pregnancy, something which she does her best to deny to herself and to others. While her condition is an unwanted one, it is also clear that her unconscious identification with the baby inside her has the potential to represent a turning point in her life, eventually allowing her to achieve some sort of cathartic recovery.

"I want my soul to fly away," Mila says, "and breathe some fresh air." Central to this process is Mila's new home, proudly made available by her good-enough adoptive (grand)parents with a generosity that stands in contrast with the failures of other significant caretakers in her life: dead or missing parents who abandoned her, and the orphanage staff who betrayed her by selling her into prostitution. Most important to Mila is her colourful bedroom, which becomes an increasingly safe shelter. The bedroom is a womb-space where, after giving birth to her child, and then as she attempts to emerge from her postpartum depression, she can recover in fantasy her good internal mother by painting her name on its walls.

Mila's other safe container is a red mobile grocery van, a kind of breast full of nourishing goodies, which had proved instrumental in her escape from her persecutor and later in her return to a more normal existence. Its friendly driver, possibly the most sensible character in the whole film despite his nutty appearance, accepts her presence in his vehicle. He may also crack a couple of not very funny jokes but he does not take advantage of her as we may have imagined him to do, nor does he even expect her to answer any of his questions. And, unlike Alex in a previous scene, he *does* stop his van when she asks him to.

I understand that one of Bulgaria's most problematic sides is its widespread corruption. It cannot be a coincidence that such a social phenomenon, so damaging to all aspects of human relationships, should also be reflected in the narrative of *Mila from Mars*. In an extended flashback sequence we are made to watch the five managers of the orphanage where Mila was a guest sitting in stern judgment (a very different chorus from the one represented by the villagers). Presumably they accept young Mila's offer of sexual favours as a means for her to avoid punishment, only to then sell her away as if she were an easily disposable object. We cannot ignore either that it is with the corrupt collusion of a border guard that the elderly peasants themselves make a living from the illegal activity of growing and smuggling cannabis.

What about the meaning of the word Mars in the film title? Not only is this the name of the Roman god of war, making us think of Mila's origins from a world full of conflict and violence, but also Mars is the name of a location somewhere out there in the universe described by Alex as almost, but not entirely, unreachable. "I want you to find her . . . even if she's gone to Mars!" he shouts to a colleague from his mobile telephone. In our collective imagination, Mars is inhabited by aliens who are not too different from us earthlings and with whom communication may one day be possible. This is consistent with the slightly uncanny sense pervading the whole movie: story, characters and locations realistic and credible, and yet also absurd and, as such, both comical and disturbing. This is exemplified, for instance, by the madness of the son of one of the villagers, described as having painted everything blue, including a donkey; or by the unorthodox situation itself of old country folk sharing a joint and smuggling drugs.

Finally, I will briefly comment on Mila's photographic activities, which are perhaps something that filmmaker Zornitsa Sophia easily identifies with; similarly, we have seen filmmaker Fernando Meirelles identifying with his character Rocket in *City of God*. Taking snapshots of her newly acquired good objects could represents Mila's way to fix in time (in the present and for the future) fleeting moments of relative happiness, making sure that she will neither forget them nor swallow them up, alongside her bad memories, into a black hole of confusion. A turning point in Mila's process of recovery occurs when she allows herself to take a picture of her son Christo. The baby is first experienced as a bad object driving her to suicidal and filicidal postpartum depression insofar as she associated him with his biological father Alex. When she allows herself to associate baby Christo (the Redeemer?) with her new and caring (if also strange) boyfriend and self-proclaimed adoptive father of her child, then the baby becomes a good-enough subject for her photographs. This young man, whom we know as "the Buddhist Teacher," is himself trying to come to terms with a traumatic war experience, but will also be instrumental in helping Mila to recover a modicum of normality in her life. His and Mila's bizarre way of getting close to each other is through an erotic face-slapping session eventually leading to a sexual relationship presumably healthier for Mila than those of her past.

Those spectators of *Mila from Mars* sitting through its end-titles (something I always do, unlike, alas, most other cinema-goers) will be rewarded by a glimpse into this newly achieved normality. In the last frames of the film, viewers are shown Mila literally in the driver's seat, having now become the grownup mother of her growing-up child. Perhaps this scene could be the prologue to a sequel still to reach our screens: a film to be entitled *The Return to Earth of Mila from Mars*.

Notes

1. *Heavenly Creatures* (New Zealand 1994). Directed by Peter Jackson. Written by Peter Jackson and Frances Walsh, based on the diaries of Pauline Parker. Starring Melanie Lynskey (Pauline) and Kate Winslet (Juliet).

2. In real life Juliet Hulme moved to Scotland, where she writes mystery novels set in Victorian times under the pen name of Anne Perry.
3. *City of God [Cidade de Deus]* (Brazil 2002). Directed by Fernando Meirelles. Written by Bráulio Mantovani, from Paulo Lins's novel. Starring Leandro Firmino (Li'l Zé) and Alexander Rodrigues (Rocket).
4. *Mila from Mars [Mila ot Mars]* (Bulgaria 2004). Directed and written by Zornitsa Sophia. Starring Vasela Kazakova (Mila), Assen Blatechki (Teacher) and Lyubomir Popov (Alex).

Chapter 5

Between eros and thanatos
Films on love

The ancient Greeks had different words to denote love. *Agapé* is a general term for its emotional component. *Filía* refers to the feelings, such as loyalty, one can have for a friend, or the affection for the members of one's family, or even the enjoyment of a specific activity. *Eros* refers to physical attraction, sensual desire and passionate love.

Such a wide range of meanings, however, is still inadequate to convey the richness and complexity of human feelings and activities subsumed under the generic term of *love*. From the infatuation of a primary school girl for her teacher to the most extreme forms of sadomasochistic sexuality, from the deep affection of a grandfather for his three-year-old grandchild to the passionate longing young lovers feel for each other . . . the list could go on and on.

Films have explored most variations on the theme of love, often throwing new light on those more bizarre and unusual aspects of it rarely considered anywhere else. Psychoanalysis, for its part, has done likewise, focusing more often on the pathological, deviant or perverse side of it than on the so-called normal one – wherever one may choose to place that most permeable of dividing lines between the two.

Drawing on the more common meaning of the Greek word "eros" to designate love, we shall look here at a few movies which portray intimate relationships, including those which have added the element of death into an already elusive concoction of love and sexuality, implying an unconscious association of loving feelings and/or sexual passion with mortality: *eros* and *thanatos*. It would, however, be naïve to expect this chapter to cover such a vast ground. All I can do here is to give some indications, with reference both to a few significant films and to a few psychoanalytic theories, about the complexity of erotic love in its multiple shades.[1]

I have identified at least three features of passionate relationships which are often represented in films dealing with them, including those discussed in this section of the book, and which call for further psychoanalytic reflections.

The first one concerns the exploration of the psychodynamic characteristics and unconscious meanings of that fine boundary which separates physical desire from emotional involvement; or, to put it more prosaically, sex from love. In particular, romantic films (much influenced by nineteenth-century literature, comedy and melodrama) can be differentiated from erotic ones in that the sexual component, while somehow present in all of them, remains mostly implicit in the former and explicit in the latter. I would add here that romantic fantasies, with their roots in infancy and their climax in adolescence, normally persist throughout life.[2] What on the other hand differentiates erotic films from pornographic ones is more difficult to determine. Definitions of which is which are couched in the subjective terms of what may be considered to be in good as opposed to bad taste (given the predominant cultural values in a particular place and time), or aesthetically pleasant as opposed to morally offensive.

The second feature emphasizes the significance of the universally recurring presence of triangular (Oedipal) constellations. Any intimate relationship between two individuals represents the enactment of powerful unconscious fantasies which include a third who is excluded from it. This is what makes such relationships and their filmic representations so exciting at times, at other times so painful, and almost always enormously complicated. Otto Kernberg (1995) points out in this connection that we can have *direct* or *reverse* triangulations; in direct triangulation the unconscious fantasy involves "an excluded third party, an idealized member of the subject's gender – the dreaded rival replicating the oedipal rival." Every man and every woman, Kernberg goes on to explain, "fears the presence of somebody who would be more satisfactory to his or her . . . partner; this third party is the origin of emotional insecurity in sexual intimacy." Reverse triangulation, on the other hand, "defines the compensating, revengeful fantasy of involvement with a person other than one's partner, an idealized member of the other gender who stands for the desired oedipal object" (Kernberg 1995, pp. 87–88).

The third aspect of erotic relationships often present in these films refers to the idealization of love objects, or rather of the real and fantasized activities involved in the process of relating to them. Love often manifests itself as a desire for interpersonal fusion, an attempt to overcome our sense of separateness (Fromm 1957). But, much as the first love affair between baby and mother has to be given in its original form, "every loving relationship has the seeds of failure within it, in so far as it expects a total return to a primordial state of unity" (Verhaege 1998, p. 50). This inevitable failure is what romance denies and replaces with an idealization: not so much of the love object himself or herself (always replaceable, more or less easily), but of the very process of falling, or of being, in love. Such a process finds its expression in real life (and is reproduced in literature and cinema) in all sorts of ways. It can take the shape of flirting, of courting, of getting physically and/ or emotionally close, of risking rejection, of exposing oneself to ridicule or pain, of the excitement of seducing and of being seduced, of rescuing and of being rescued, of the joys but also the potential disappointment (always lurking behind the corner) of having one's longings fulfilled, not to mention those constant doubts so beautifully expressed by Zerlina's aria ("*Vorrei e non vorrei . . .*" – "*I would and I would not . . .*") in Mozart's *Don Giovanni*. Ultimately, the driving force behind all romantic and erotic narratives is the fairy-tale fantasy, "*and they lived happily ever after*," an updated version of that nostalgic wish to remain forever in a state of blissful symbiotic fusion inside the maternal womb.

It almost goes without saying that all of the above is underscored by the phenomenon of transference – the repetition in present love relationships of past scenarios and psychodynamics, involving the utilization of such unconscious mental processes as regression to childhood patterns of interaction, denial of present interpersonal realities, displaced attribution to current partners of characteristics belonging to others, and so on. While transference (with its complementary side, the countertransference) is normally only observed and interpreted within the walls of our consulting rooms, the phenomenon is universal as it applies to all human relationships, and with an intensity and significance directly proportional to their degree of intimacy and emotional potency.

As an instance of a film touching on some of these issues I will briefly mention here Luchino Visconti's *Ossessione*,[3] a torrid love story between Giovanna (Clara Calamai) and Gino (Massimo Girotti), a handsome but unreliable drifter. They will end up killing her hated husband, only to then pay the highest price for their crime. Based on James M. Cain's novel *The Postman Always Rings Twice* (Cain 1934) and relocated to the desolate lowlands of the Po Delta in northern Italy, *Ossessione* is a film about sensual passion and guilt, about crime and self-punishment, about loyalty and betrayal.[4] It is also a film imbued with rich variations on the Oedipal theme. Two symmetrical characters, challenging the traditional family triangle of parents and child (or at least the fantasy of it), intrude in its narrative: the Spagnolo, a young man who develops an ambiguously homoerotic attachment to Gino, representing for him an Ideal Ego and model of identification, but who then becomes his betrayer; and Anita, the tart-with-a-heart (see Chapter Two) who seduces Gino but also tries to rescue him from his troubles.

Giovanna deludes herself that she can reconstitute the nuclear family through the birth of a child. She believes that, having become pregnant, she and Gino are now morally entitled to a happy existence and to freedom from their guilt because the forthcoming birth of their baby will compensate for the murder of her old husband (a father figure). Yet she should know, and will soon find out, that the elimination of the third – be it out of love, jealousy or greed – could never bring happiness or peace to the other two. Émile Zola's classic novel *Thérèse Raquin* (1867) is a good literary illustration of this principle, and *Double Indemnity* (Billy Wilder 1944) is the classic *film noir* on that same topic. Or, to express it in more psychoanalytic terms: the regression to the pre-Oedipal fantasy of a symbiotic union with the mother is not a valid solution to our Oedipal complex dilemmas.

*****

Directed by 32-year-old Belgian filmmaker Frédéric Fonteyne and impeccably played by Nathalie Baye and Sergi López (an actor we have already met in *Pan's Labyrinth* in Chapter Three), *A Pornographic Affair*[5] belongs to a Gallic tradition of post-Nouvelle Vague, postexistentialist romantic films which explore, in the footsteps of such directors as Truffaut, Rivette and Rohmer, the nooks and crooks of close relationships.[6]

It is an adult story intended for adult viewers. Its adult protagonists are two credible, decent individuals who, drawn to each other for sexual purposes, end up falling in love. Without much of the *pruderie* that might have been problematic to a younger couple ("Look," the female lead character tells her interviewer, "at my age I can talk freely about sex"), what they find instead most difficult to come to terms with is the unexpectedly intense, almost violent emotional side of their relationship.

Aptly described by a critic as "a magnificent meditation upon the mutability of human desires and emotions" (Berardinelli 2000), Fonteyne's film is built around an in-depth analytical exploration, accurate to the point of being hurtful, of the transformations of the relationship between a man and a woman, gradually crossing the boundaries from perversity to normality (not the other way round, as would be expected in a more conventional erotic story); from purely physical sexuality to requited love.

At the risk of appearing pedantic, I must say that I am intrigued by this film's original French title *Une Liaison pornographique*. Not just because it is misleading, this one not being at all a pornographic movie, but also because the word pornography literally refers to the *representation* of sexuality.[7] A more accurate title could then perhaps be *Une Liaison erotique*, or *Une Liaison perverse*. However, while disapproving of such an incorrect choice of the word pornography, I shall not refrain from using it myself in this chapter, on the grounds that it is the film's protagonist herself who describes her affair as pornographic. I will add that American distributors, probably out of a mixture of moral cowardice and commercial expediency rather than philological sophistication, translated this film's title as *An Affair of Love*. This made me consider whether perhaps romantic films (such as this) are not simply what is left behind after you have removed the pornographic scenes from them.

As I have suggested, intimate relationships (whether portrayed in romantic literature and cinema, or experienced in real life) are often characterized by a sustained tension between sexual desire and emotional involvement. This could not be stated (or, rather, be questioned) more clearly than in the simple narrative of *A Pornographic Affair*. The film consists of a number of scenes featuring a couple, simply named (but we only learn this from the end-titles) as Elle and Lui: waiting for each other and then conversing in *their* Paris café; getting the key to *their* room in a nearby hotel for a session of sexual pleasures; standing among the crowd in a street surrounded by traffic and failing to find an easy way to part at the end of each encounter. These wonderfully crafted sequences, which give meticulous attention to the smallest details of expression, gesture, speech and mannerism, are intercut with clips from interviews conducted with Elle and Lui at an unspecified time after the end of their affair, by a calm, disembodied male voice, like that of an analyst sitting unseen behind the couch. (We have already encountered an instance of it in Hugh Brody's film *Nineteen Nineteen* [see Chapter 1] where Freud is not seen but his voice can be heard off-screen as the camera focuses on his patients lying on his couch.)

The off-screen interviewer is interested in finding out the deeper emotional meaning of their liaison (a term, by the way, which unlike *affair* implies a link, a tie, or a bond) and not at all in trying to pass moral judgment on it. The interviewer's identity is not revealed to us: perhaps he stands for the film's director himself, searching for answers instead of having to decide what they should be in order to make his movie. Or perhaps he is any of us spectators, hoping to discover the facts instead of being left with the realization that we should learn to leave our childish curiosity about the Primal Scene unfulfilled, and to tolerate (as psychoanalysts like to term it) the anxiety of not knowing. This realization is more frustrating but also more rewarding than our answer-digging, because it is closer to the truth.

There is perhaps an interesting coincidence in the fact that Elle is played by the experienced actress Nathalie Baye. As well as having starred in some sixty films, including Truffaut's *Day for Night* (1973) and Godard's *Sauve qui peut* (1980), Baye also played the role of Gérard Depardieu's wife Bertrande in Daniel Vigne's *Le Retour de Martin Guerre* (1982). In that film, set in sixteenth-century rural France, Bertrande accepts Martin as her husband returning after nine years in the war while many others in the village (and the spectators with them) are left uncertain as to his identity, for there is evidence that he may be just a cunning look-alike impostor. She knows the truth, of course, sharing with him all bedroom intimacies, and he knows that she knows it, but *we* are left in the dark. We only know, as it were, that they know and that they are not going to tell us.

Similarly, in *A Pornographic Affair* we also know the protagonists are privy to a truth about themselves from which we, the audience, are deliberately excluded. We are presented, in fact, with what film critic Roger Ebert calls "a void to tantalize our imaginations" (2000), with that *manque* (or *lack*) which Lacan considers to be the necessary ingredient of desire: once you fill that void up, by letting fantasy be replaced by its fulfillment, desire disappears altogether.

It is indeed in the nature of art to distance us from reality, while pretending to get us engaged with it; and, as Christian Metz (1974) reminds us, doubly so in the case of cinema. Its peculiar fascination stems from the fact that it never offers us real objects, but only representations of them (actually, just a reflection of their representation). What we see on the screen, in other words, are the fictional Elle and Lui, not the real Nathalie Baye and Sergi López, until we realize that even the Elle and Lui whom we believe we are seeing are not actual people (as they would be, say, on a theatre stage) but just shadows and lights projected on a screen at the end of a semidark room. I hardly need to remind my readers here of Plato's description (in his *Republic*) of the Myth of the Cave; cinema may be, like psychoanalysis, just over a century old, but its invention goes back some two thousand and four hundred years.[8]

In Fonteyne's movie, however, we are deliberately deprived of something more. The protagonists, faced with the off-screen interviewer, refuse to answer some of his questions, which would be central to the narrative of their liaison. Like the interviewer, we are never to share their "pornographic" secrets, though we are allowed to suspect that what gives them so much pleasure is something more elaborate than the so-called missionary position. But then, as Joyce McDougall puts it, "it could be said that perversion, like beauty, is in the eye of the beholder. There is little doubt that the leading 'erotogenic zone' is located in the mind!" (McDougall 1991, p. 178). Like the curious child still alive and kicking inside all of us, we are left in the company of Fonteyne's camera, discreetly waiting outside the parental bedroom. Breaking the unbearable visual silence in front of us, we watch a chambermaid pushing her trolley full of linen along the hotel corridor. That's all we are allowed to see. The door of room N° 118 remains firmly shut in front of us.

If this undoubtedly frustrates our voyeuristic needs, emotionally and intellectually we are left, I think, deeply satisfied. As I have already suggested, *A Pornographic Affair* is not, after all, a pornographic film, even if what takes place between its protagonists is described by Elle in the initial interview as a *pornographique* affair. Her statement, "We were there just for the sex," applies perhaps to herself and her lover, but not to us, the viewers. Furthermore, much as the film excludes its audience from their secret, Lui and Elle also deliberately deprive each other of those fragments of identity (name, age, marital status, job) which, as they rightly suspect, could only interfere with their fantasies. Maybe they have been to the movies and seen Bernardo Bertolucci's *Last Tango in Paris* (1972), another masterpiece on intimate but anonymous liaisons (perhaps intimate *because* anonymous), set in the same city as Fonteyne's film. Maybe they have themselves been sitting behind a psychoanalytic couch (as we don't know their profession, we are left free to speculate that either, or both, may be colleagues of ours), or lying on one as analysands, and may thus have learned how useful it is for therapists to maintain an attitude of neutrality. What is more likely, though, is that they have some unconscious knowledge that, were they to start talking about aspects of their personal existences foreign to themselves as a couple, they would end up inserting that Oedipal third element which could destabilize their otherwise blissful illusion of a regressive, purely sensual, one-to-one liaison, undisturbed by jealousy and envy. Paradoxically, however, it is the very absence of such a third object that makes its potential presence profoundly felt throughout the film: a kind of very loud visual silence.

This silence becomes explicit when, in lateral counterpoint to the story of our couple, another story is sketched out in the film which introduces an element of external reality, a toxic component as dangerous as it is unavoidable, into their anonymity. An elderly gentleman, Monsieur Ligneaux (we are told *his* name), collapses almost literally on their doorstep, and will be taken to die, of all places, in that same hospital, la Salpêtrière, where in 1885 Freud had attended Jean Martin Charcot's lectures on hysteria. Monsieur Ligneaux's loving attempt to protect his wife from the news of his terminal condition fails; he has remained emotionally though not sexually faithful to her, and we will later learn from a newspaper article that she has already committed suicide. Elle and Lui are, again, powerless when faced with the power of love.

As its narrative progresses, *A Pornographic Affair* becomes a profound meditation on intimate communication itself. How do I share my private thoughts and

Figure 5.1 Nathalie Baye and Sergi López in *A Pornographic Affair* (Fonteyne 1999)

feelings with another person – a parent, a sister, a lover, or indeed a psychoanalyst? How do I know that I am not misunderstanding or being misunderstood? Although misunderstanding does not always lead to tragic consequences (like it famously does in *Romeo and Juliet*), it can still induce a sense of profound isolation and loneliness, even in a couple engaged in an otherwise intimate relationship.

At one crucial moment towards the end of the film we watch Lui and Elle in their café, facing each other in pensive, near-to-tears silence. The filmic medium allows us to hear him thinking: *"I was in love. . . . And then I knew. She didn't want to. She wanted to stop. She hadn't said anything but it was obvious. I could read her face."*

Lui says: "Between the two of us . . . It won't work".

Almost without realizing the enormity of that statement, Elle replies: "No."

Then we hear her thoughts: *"I had decided to stay with him. . . . But when he said that the two of us . . . wouldn't work, it seemed obvious. He was right. We had to split up. . . . I could see that he wanted to stop it. So I wanted that too."*

The interviewer asks the most devastating of questions about their relationship, or rather about their decision to end it: "What if it was a mistake?" How easy it is for Lui to assume that Elle wants him only because he wants her! Or that Elle wants their relationship to finish only because he is afraid that it may continue!

Through the device of the flash-forward interview at the beginning of the film, Fonteyne bribes us into not complaining of our enforced ignorance by offering us spectators a crucial element of information about our couple which they themselves still ignore in the course of the few months of their affair: we know, and they (at least consciously) do not, that it is going to come to an end. This creates in us a sense of closure. If ultimately it never feels really disappointing it is only because, throughout the film, we can still foolishly hope, disavowing our own perceptions, that the pornographic, or romantic, affair between Elle and Lui may somehow continue. As they get to know one another, we, their audience, also get to know them and to like them. Maybe we even identify with them. And maybe we want them to find for themselves that same kind of happiness in intimacy that all of us keep seeking in our own lives.

Films such as *A Pornographic Affair* can have an unexpectedly powerful emotional impact on their spectators. This may be simply because, by presenting us credible characters in all their contradictory complexities, they allow us to recognize them as being truly real. This is in contrast with so many dramatically sentimental, but ultimately superficial, big stories which have conditioned us to identify with idealized, superhuman heroes only existing in the overstretched imagination of the filmmakers who have created them and in the fantasies of increasingly passive audiences.

In the course of my reflections on some of the features of Frédéric Fonteyne's film, I have made reference to a number of psychoanalytically informed ideas, such as (a) triangular constellations; (b) the analytic function of the interviewer in relation to Lui and Elle; (c) the regressive tendency towards interpersonal fusion; (d) the spectators' frustrated voyeuristic fantasies about the unseen pornographic components of the main characters' love affair; and (e) the ultimate *incommunicability* (to borrow a neologism used in relation to films by such *auteurs* as Antonioni, Bergman or Godard) between human beings that sometimes leads to tragic misunderstandings, and always to a sense of great loneliness. Having drawn on such ideas, I hope to have at least succeeded in reminding my readers of the existence of another intimate relationship: the one that allows psychoanalysis and cinema to approach, cross-fertilize, and enrich each other.

****

Another component of love relationships providing the narrative backbone to many films is the fantasy that one's erotic attachment has the power to *rescue* the other (and, in the process, oneself) from his or her unhappy condition, whatever the latter may be.

Since its earliest days our psychoanalytic profession has emerged not just, or even not so much, as a form of treatment of neurotic or other mental conditions, but as a theoretically, technically and ethically organized attempt to recover, out of that huge reservoir we call the Unconscious, something apparently gone lost, dead or mad. In other words, the psychoanalytic endeavour itself could be described as a vast rescue operation. This is metaphorically represented by Freud as an archaeological exploration of the mind. He writes: "[The analyst's] work of construction, or, if it is preferred, of reconstruction resembles to a great extent an archaeologist's excavation of some dwelling-place that has been destroyed and buried. . . . The two processes are in fact identical, except that the analyst works under better conditions and has more material at his command to assist him, since what he is dealing with is *not something destroyed but something that is still alive*. . . . Both of them have an undisputed right to reconstruct by means of supplementing and combining the surviving remains" (Freud 1937b, p. 259; my emphasis).

The psychoanalytic process of recovery could then be seen as an instance of those powerful rescue fantasies which manifest themselves in many forms and shapes, depending on any of numerous factors. For example, the fantasy may involve an element of self-sacrifice on the part of the rescuer (the organ donor), sometimes to the extreme of risking his or her own life (the freedom-fighter). The fantasy may depend on the presence of an ambition not just to save or salvage, but also to convert the rescued (literally so in the religious missionary programs); or on what it is that one is rescuing oneself or others from – usually some real or imagined danger, illness, evil, sin, ignorance, or death; and, most importantly, on the specific combination and interplay of conscious and unconscious components.

We can find manifestations of rescue fantasies in numerous aspects of everyday life, for instance in our choice of friends and sexual partners, or in our career choice, be it social work, plastic surgery, tapestry restoration, or ecology lecturing. However much we try and rationalize them, unconscious transference factors involving the reenactment of earlier scenarios will always be influential in such choices of relationships and activities.

It goes without saying that, regardless of their unconscious motivation and of the fantasies underlying their performance, most rescuing acts are highly valued by society and include some of the noblest (and, occasionally, most misconceived) deeds in the history of our discontented civilization. These are, in Kleinian terminology, reparative gestures intended to assuage the sense of guilt stemming from primitive destructive fantasies against the mother's body. Rescue fantasies can find expression in either active or passive forms, depending on whether we see ourselves as subjects or objects of salvage operations: we may be committed to nursing disabled children, or we may be those accident-prone individuals to be met with uncanny regularity in the local hospital's accident and emergency department. We shall, however, not be surprised to find both the active and the passive versions combined in the same person (an accident-prone nurse!). This is acknowledged in psychoanalytic training protocols, which require prospective practitioners to first undergo their own training analysis: to be rescued themselves before they qualify to rescue others. Indeed, active and passive rescue fantasies are present in all psychoanalytic consulting rooms, where analysts consciously strive to relieve their analysands' suffering and unconsciously hope also to relieve their own through it (Greenacre 1966). At the same time, analysands often wish to save, alongside themselves, their analysts (Grinstein 1957; Searles 1975), whom they may perceive as being weak and helpless wounded healers.

In a clinical context, Atwood (1978) understands what he calls "messianic salvation fantasies" as reactions to traumatic childhood experiences of disappointment and loss. Another special case of rescue fantasy to be encountered in our work concerns the process of mourning and the not-infrequent attempt on the part of parents who have lost a child to replace (that is, bring magically back to life) the lost little girl or boy by soon conceiving another one. Such replacement children may develop psychological problems, especially in the area of self-identity, as they grow up with the sense that their parents expect them to be someone other than themselves (Sabbadini 1988).

Whatever their original features, however, rescue fantasies often include among their overdetermined sources a component of unresolved narcissistic infantile omnipotence with its related primitive delusional ideas of immortality.[9] These, in turn, have the role of defenses (through a process of conversion into their opposites) stemming from, respectively, the dependence of children upon caring adults and from the reality of our biological condition as mortals. In this connection, Freud refers to the "rescue motif" and speculates on its psychogenic significance as "an independent derivative of the . . . parental complex." He explains: "When a child hears that he owes his life to his parents, or that his mother gave him life, his feelings of tenderness unite with impulses which strive at power and independence, and they generate the wish to return this gift to the parents and to repay them with one of equal value. It is as though the boy's defiance were to make him say: 'I want nothing from my father; I will give him back all I have cost him.' He then forms the phantasy of rescuing his father from danger and saving his life; in this way he puts his account square with him. . . . In its application to a boy's father it is the defiant meaning in the idea of rescuing which is by far the most important; where his mother is concerned it is usually its tender meaning. The mother gave the child life, and it is not easy to find a substitute of equal value for this unique gift" (Freud 1910b, pp. 172–173). Abraham (1922) further develops the Oedipal theme of the rescue of the father by noticing the concomitant element of aggression against him, also emphasised by Sterba (1940), while Frosch (1959) explores rescue fantasies in the wider context of Family Romance fantasies as they emerge in the analytic transference.[10]

A superb illustration of several mutually intersecting rescue fantasies is provided by the Mexican film *Amores Perros* (2000).[11] It begins with a shocking car accident which brings into close proximity the lives of otherwise unrelated characters.[12] Around the pivotal narrative crossroads of this dramatic opening sequence, *Amores Perros*, described in an interview by its director as "a visceral film that shouts all the time," introduces us to several of the events surrounding the motor crash. Cleverly narrated in nonlinear fashion through brilliant editing and with the help of flashbacks and flash-forwards, the plot unravels in three parallel, yet interconnected, episodes or chapters where characters from one appear in, or pass through, another. On one occasion, for instance, the sense of continuity is provided by characters of the second episode taking part in a television program which is being watched by some of the protagonists of the first one.

The three main stories take place in present-day Mexico City. The first one revolves around the frustrated desire of a young man to run away with his sister-in-law; the second one is about the physical, moral and psychological dissolution of a beautiful woman; and the last narrative concerns the attempts of a mysterious tramp to get back in touch with his long-lost daughter. All three stories are drenched with transgressive passions, almost intolerable violence, and profound humanity.

A variety of critical readings and interpretative keys is available to those wishing to gain access to at least some of the multiple meanings of this film. For instance, one might want to understand *Amores Perros* by concentrating on the sociopolitical, moral and philosophical messages which it tries to convey. Alternatively, some critics may try and locate this movie historically within the tradition of Mexican cinema or of the recent Latin American *Buena Onda*; within particular cinematic genres, such as melodrama or gangster narratives; or through a comparison with other films, for example Quentin Tarantino's influential *Pulp Fiction* (1994). Other viewers may want to emphasize instead the formal aspects of Iñárritu's work, such as his frequent use of handheld camera shots to give the film an almost documentary feel, or the recurrent presence of significant still photographs of all sizes and shapes – pictures to be found in albums, frames and wallets; on newspapers, billboards and walls – as a device to freeze time in contrast with the often furious pace of the action.

Even if we restricted our approach to a psychoanalytically oriented perspective, we would still have several options available to us. For instance, we could choose for this critical exercise to focus on such a theme as, say, the developmental origins in the oral-cannibalistic stage of the greed that motivates the behaviour of so many characters – men, women and dogs. Instead, I would like to present here a psychoanalytically informed analysis of selected aspects of this film's narrative. More specifically, I intend to structure my comments around the recurrent theme of rescue fantasies, in the hope that our understanding of *Amores Perros* may be enriched by this particular approach. In order to do this, however, we must first make a detour into other cultural territories.

Popular narratives, from the Old Testament prototypical story of Noah's Ark onwards, are frequently built around the rescue motif.[13] This motif can also be found in a number of Greek legends,[14] notably in that of Theseus and Ariadne. Here I would like to focus on the beautiful love story of Orpheus and Eurydice (better known to us in later Latin versions from the first century BC). As a metaphor of our deepest fears, desires and conflicts, this story is also relevant to the analytic understanding of many psychological phenomena (Bonaparte 1954). The most common version of the myth goes as follows:

> *Eurydice, bride of the famous poet, singer and musician Orpheus, is fatally bitten by a snake. Orpheus, relying on the power of his art, descends to Hades to rescue her back to the world of the living and persuades the gods of the Underworld to relinquish her, but finally loses her again when he disobeys their command not to look back towards her before they reemerge from Hades.*[15]

Classical interpretations vary concerning the crucial moment when Orpheus turns his gaze towards Eurydice, thus causing her second death and his final loss of her. For Virgil (Fourth *Georgic*) this impulsive gesture is due to a moment of madness,

what he calls *furor* or *dementia*. Ovid, on the other hand, attributes it to the caring concern of a husband for his wife's weakness – as well as to his own greedy
passion. Writes Ovid:

> *Hic, ne deficeret, metuens avidusque videndi flexit amans oculos, et protinus*
> *illa relapsa est.* (He, afraid that she might fail and greedy of seeing her, in
> love turned back his eyes and at once she slipped back.)
>
> *(Metamorphoses*, 10: 56–57)

From a psychoanalytic perspective, I would suggest two alternative explanations
for Orpheus's irrational and (self-)destructive gesture. If his journey to the Underworld represents a regressive immersion into the Unconscious, a mental space dominated by Primary Process functioning, he would as a consequence behave according
to the Pleasure Principle. In other words Orpheus, like a hungry baby incapable
of tolerating delays to the gratification of his needs, would become a victim to his
own greed and turn his head back before the reasonable time imposed on him by
the gods, representing here the demands of external reality and his own superego.

The other explanation for Orpheus's behaviour may rest on his unconscious
sense of guilt for daring to break a taboo, that is, for upsetting the natural order of
things whereby the dead must be left to rest forever *(Let sleeping dogs lie)*, and
for using his position as an artist to extort privileges from the gods. Much as he
wants to rescue Eurydice, his superego does not allow him in the end to carry out
his mission; he therefore unconsciously sabotages it by plunging his beloved back
where she truly, if of course also tragically, belongs.[16]

Furthermore, his encounter with Eurydice in the shadowy World of the Dead
has the basic structure of a romantic love story, and a doomed one to boot *(Man*
fights to conquer the woman of his dreams, seems to succeed against all odds,
until tragedy destroys their happiness), with the universal appeal that such narratives have, for they represent everyone's deepest and most regressive fears and
desires. Orpheus and Eurydice, in other words, while remaining beyond mankind's reach, are at the same time idealized versions of us, as they let us project
aspects of ourselves into them.

This myth's power, I suggest, stems from a complex structure or pattern: that
basic rescue motif which, as I have indicated, is the motor force behind many of
our wishes and behaviours. Rescue fantasies, whereby the Self achieves relief
from an unbearable sense of guilt, may then constitute attempts to deal with all
sorts of unconsciously desired, or even enacted, violations to the natural order
of things, including the Oedipal crimes of murder and incest. In the case of the
Orpheus myth we could perhaps find here an even deeper wish: that eros in combination with art (Orpheus's love for Eurydice combined with his musical capacity to move even the gods) – or, to put it more psychoanalytically, libido combined
with sublimation – could eventually defeat thanatos.

So, in fact, we are back to our unconscious and universal wish for immortality
expressed by the concept "not something destroyed but something that is still

alive." I emphasized this concept above when quoting Freud (1937b): "if only Orpheus had not turned around to look at his Eurydice." But the thought, rational as it appears to be (indeed, as we have said, even Virgil attributes Orpheus's impulse to his dementia, or folly), is naïve. Much as you cannot teach an old dog new tricks, human beings never entirely abandon the Pleasure Principle in favour of the Reality one. Whether because of lust or greed, impatience or passion, we regularly (some more frequently than others) end up behaving in ways that contradict our best intentions and interests. To make things worse, we also feel compelled (again, some more frequently than others) to neurotically repeat our mistakes. Our dementia, then, is but a fundamental incapacity to learn from experience. Having lost Eurydice once, Orpheus must lose her again.[17]

I would argue that the three main narratives in *Amores Perros*, as well as its overall meaning, are constructed at the intersection of desperate and unsuccessful rescue attempts.

The first episode is ferociously fast and powerful. A young man, Octavio/ Orpheus (Gael García Bernal), falls in passionate and dangerous love with his sister-in-law Susana/Eurydice (Vanessa Bauche) – another incestuous variation, no doubt, on the Oedipus theme. He is trying to protect her and her child from her abusive husband Ramiro, who is Octavio's own brother[18] and, we may suggest, the döppelganger dark side of himself. We see Ramiro come back home, insult Susana who is holding the child on her lap, and blame her for having let Cofi the dog out of the house. "Where's that fucking dog?" he asks her aggressively. She looks scared, yet also accustomed to that sort of abuse. "You let him out again, right, bitch?" insists Ramiro, ready to hit her. And here his brother intervenes, showing us for the first time his rescuing attitude. Indifferent to Ramiro's claim that "This is between me and my wife," Octavio takes the blame upon himself: "I'm the one," he says, "who let the dog go, so lay off her." "Keep out of it," answers Ramiro, but he leaves the kitchen, conceding defeat at least in this first confrontation.

It will soon emerge that Octavio fantasizes about running away with Susana (now pregnant again) and her baby, a scheme about which she feels most ambivalent. He plans to save the money needed for their elopement by making their rottweiler Cofi fight in the bloody arenas of illegal dog-fighting and betting.[19] "This'll be our bank, OK?" Octavio tells her, as he stashes his cash in her suitcase. "Just yours and mine. . . . This money's clean, so you'll come away with me." "Come away with you?" she asks, incredulous.

In the context of our mythical interpretation, the all-evil character of Ramiro possibly represents the snake that had bitten Eurydice to death or the gods who keep her prisoner in the Underworld – guarded, it may be interesting to notice, by a monstrous three-headed *perro*, Cerberus. Indeed, the flat in the outskirts of the city where they all live together (the two brothers, their mother, Susana, her baby and the rottweiler) sharing a cramped space in an atmosphere of near-exploding tension, has many features of an urban hell; though, admittedly, one more similar to Dante's noisy Inferno than to the Greeks' own Hades, or Kingdom of the

Invisible, populated as it was by quiet ghostly shadows. (Which of these two, I wonder, would the darkest corners of the Unconscious resemble? We are not to know.)

Eventually, like Orpheus, Octavio finds out that he has failed in his rescue mission when Susana, whom we meet again in the final episode of *Amores Perros* at Ramiro's funeral, decides to remain faithful to her husband's memory and does not turn up to meet Octavio at the bus station. Reality has caught up with the dream. "You don't get it, do you?" he asks her several times throughout the film. Obstacles cannot always be overcome by our desires. Love has not prevailed: this is not Hollywood, after all! Having first found his Eurydice, Octavio, now badly scarred by the motor accident which has left him on crutches, has to relinquish her again. It is for us almost physically painful to watch him so utterly distraught by that experience of loss, as if his whole life had come to a premature end.

Unlike the first "chapter," which is about a story leading up to the car crash we had witnessed at the beginning of the film, and the third one which will recount events that follow it, the second episode of *Amores Perros* takes place in the present time of the accident. Relying on a filmic language that alternates black satire with drama, this love story between a beautiful top model and her new partner is also a bitter reflection on the superficiality of the worlds of media and advertisement. Their success, Iñárritu seems to tell us, rests on deception, and their wealth depends on a poverty of moral values.

The publisher Daniel (Álvaro Guerrero), whom we have already met with his family in the film's first episode, has just separated from his wife and abandoned his young daughters in order to be with Valeria (Goya Toledo). He gives her the surprise present of a luxurious love-nest in town, but, as it happens, little happiness is in store for them there. As a result of the road accident, Valeria's brilliant career and fragile mental balance are shattered when she finds herself bound to a wheelchair, her right leg imprisoned in a metal brace.[20] Then another loss throws Valeria into a state of overwhelming anxiety, hysterical frenzy and impotent rage when her pet dog Richie/Eurydice, her baby-self to whom she is bonded in regressively symbiotic identification, falls through a hole in the floor and disappears under it. This symbolic space is yet another representation of the Underworld, and therefore of the Unconscious too. The space in this instance is populated (in Valeria's morbid fantasy, if not in reality) by "thousands of rats," or dangerous demons, intensifying the castration anxiety already mobilized within her by her injury. Daniel tries his best to help, but his vain efforts only make her increasingly furious and him frustrated, until the pressure becomes intolerable and explodes in a dramatic bedroom dogfight between them: "Get Richie out!" she shouts at him. "He can get himself out!" he retorts, getting up from their bed. "You faggot! You've always been selfish!" Valeria screams, her beautiful face now distorted by fury and pain. "I gave up everything for you!" pleads Daniel. "Yeah," she answers, full of venom, "your bitchy wife and stupid daughters!" "Shut up or I'll hit you!" he says in exasperation. "You piece of shit!" shouts Valeria, and Daniel: "Go fuck yourself, you and your fucking dog!" Exit Daniel. Valeria overdoses.

The final devastating blow to her narcissistic self-image, brought about by the amputation of her leg, leaves Valeria's psychological state in tatters. With it goes her modeling career, which lacks the potentially reparative force of creativity, dependent as it is instead on little more than skin-deep beauty. Even if Daniel/Orpheus, after much display of anguish, hammering and destruction of floorboards, will eventually recover Valeria's dog from down under, it is obvious that Valeria herself is by now beyond rescue. Although this story, like the other two in *Amores Perros,* is left open-ended, we know the gradual disintegration of Valeria's life has reached its final stages when we see the gigantic sexy posters of her advertising the "Enchant" brand of perfume getting torn down throughout the city. Frightened and depressed, she has fallen back into an unreachable rat-infested Underworld.

In the final episode of *Amores Perros,* which has the structure and flavour of a spiritual journey, we discover some disturbing truths about El Chivo (Emilio Echevarría), a character we had already met several times earlier in the film. We know him from the first episodes as an old tramp who roams the city with his several stray dogs (including, by now, Octavio's rottweiler, whom he has rescued from the car accident), and who earns a living as a gun-for-hire. Gradually we discover a more complex truth about him: as a young man Chivo had been a politically engaged intellectual who had abandoned his wife and child to become a revolutionary guerrilla, until he was caught and sentenced to twenty years in jail.

Through the mediation of the same corrupt cop who had originally arrested him, Chivo is now offered by businessman Gustavo/Cain the job of assassinating his half-brother and partner, Luis/Abel. The murderous hostile brothers are graphically presented here like two greedy dogs facing each other and ready to fight for their lives in the ring: *Homo homini lupus* – the *lupus* (wolf) being a close relative of the *canis* (dog). We had of course already encountered a similar

Figure 5.2 Emilio Echevarria in *Amores Perros* (Iñárritu 2000)

scenario in the first part of the film, dominated by the dog-eat-dog hatred between brothers Octavio and Ramiro.

Taking advantage of the tragicomic situation created by the double kidnapping of Gustavo and Luis, which includes the acquisition of a large amount of money, Chivo tries to get back in touch with his adored adolescent daughter Maru. His doomed attempt to recover and reconnect with her provides the main emotional tension in this final love story. Maru/Eurydice had not seen her father Chivo/ Orpheus since she was a two-year-old child. He had at the time agreed with his wife that she would be telling the young girl he had died instead of revealing to her the potentially more disturbing truth. His tragedy is that he had committed those political crimes that separate him from his family in the hope he could offer her daughter a better future. "I wanted to set the world right," he confesses on her answering machine, "and then share it with you. . . . I failed, as you can see."

He resurfaces at his wife's funeral, a turning point in his story like Ramiro's had been in Octavio's life, but still remaining incognito to Maru. It is remarkable, incidentally, that he should become so obsessed with his daughter at this particular time, as if he had to wait until his estranged wife had passed away before fulfilling his Oedipal dream. To all intents and purposes he had been, in his own words, "a living ghost" for Maru insofar as she had never known he was still alive. He accomplishes his rescue mission of leaving the illicitly obtained amount of cash under her pillow and, as his swan song (Orpheus-the-musician again!), a message of paternal love: "I swore to your mother I'd never try to see you again . . . but I couldn't do it." Then Chivo walks away again from her life, presumably forever, to spare her further suffering: "I'll be back to find you," he tells her on the telephone between tears, "once I have the courage to look you in the eyes." These could well have been Orpheus's words to his wife: but, in the Greek myth, it was precisely because he *did* have the courage, or the madness, to look Eurydice in the eyes that he lost her. Chivo, whom we have compared to Orpheus in his attempts to recover his girl, can also then be seen as the one who, Eurydice-like, briefly comes back to life in the present only to be gone again without being even recognized by his Maru. Chivo's last words to her, "I love you, my little girl," are uttered after the bleep of her answering machine has cut him off.

In the last scene of the film we see the backs of Chivo and his dog Cofi walking away from us in a bleak, almost surreal suburban landscape. Then, before the end-titles, we read on a black background the dedication of *Amores Perros* to the memory of Luciano, one of its actors who died before the film was completed: "Because we are also what we have lost."

I have so far made only passing references to the dogs. Yet, director Iñárritu often places them at the very centre (and in the title) of his film, alongside its human protagonists. Is he trying to tell us here that human beings are as bad as *perros* or, quite the opposite, that the world would be a better place if only we behaved as honestly as man's best friends do? After all, they have a reputation for remaining loyal to their masters even when they are only given a dog's life instead of the one they deserve; and indeed many people believe they can relate better to their animals than they can to fellow human beings.

In the end, with the exception of Valeria's lap-pet Richie, the only character in *Amores Perros* to be rescued without being lost again is the rottweiler Cofi, possibly the film's true protagonist: an animal so fierce that not even Orpheus would have been able to tame him, and perhaps a reminder of Iñárritu's cynicism[21] about the true nature of *homo sapiens*. Already on the road to death in the first sequence of the film and risking his life many times in fights with other dogs, Cofi proves to be a born survivor, thus reinforcing his owner's unconscious omnipotent fantasies. Having provided Octavio with the money to fulfill his transgressive dream, eventually aborted, to run away with Susana (that is, having done for his owner something similar to what the lyre had done for Orpheus when he had played it to seduce the gods of Hades), Cofi will find in Chivo his new master. As I have mentioned before, the tramp had rescued him from the crucial road accident that structures all the stories in the film. But later, having lovingly nursed Cofi back to health, Chivo discovers that during his absence the fierce dog had bitten all his other pets to death. Upset and enraged, with tears filling his eyes, Chivo prepares to shoot Cofi in revenge. However, in a last-minute gesture of concern, perhaps realizing that Cofi could not be blamed for having done what, after all, is in his canine nature, he rescues the animal from his own wrath by sparing his life for a second time (whereas Eurydice had died twice).[22]

In conclusion, my critical understanding of Iñárritu's film *Amores Perros* along psychoanalytic lines has developed into an exploration of various meanings of the rescue fantasy. This fantasy is a universally common and important complex, part conscious and part unconscious, and is often related to our primary narcissism, violations of Oedipal taboos and primitive fantasies of immortality. This exploration has involved looking at occurrences of the rescue fantasy, including some of its artistic representations, in a variety of intrapsychic and interpersonal scenarios. In particular, I have made reference to the fascinating Greek myth of Orpheus and Eurydice as an instance of the emotional impact such fantasies can have, notwithstanding the passing of time, through the centuries. The analysis of certain crucial events in the film has allowed us to relate some of its characters and their behaviours to that story, and has shown that *Amores Perros* is a remarkably eloquent contemporary illustration of it.

Orpheus and Eurydice's classical story of love and loss teaches us, among other things, that much as we want to believe that we are the architects of our own destiny *(Homo faber est suae quisque fortunae)*, our frailty makes us powerless, *pace* psychoanalysis, ultimately to affect it. This darkly pessimistic view of mankind is echoed in Iñárritu's film by a piece of Mexican folk wisdom; in response to Octavio, who during his brother's funeral service reminds Susana about his plan to run away with her, she comments, "My grandmother used to say, 'To make God laugh, tell him your plans.'" Fortunately God's laughter has never stopped us, and never should stop us, from making our plans and dreaming our dreams.

*****

Unlike with other *Nouvelle Vague* (New Wave) filmmakers such as Rohmer, Godard and Rivette, Claude Chabrol's work sits comfortably within mainstream cinema. His movies, enriching with subtle black comedy and social critique the psychological thriller genre, often deal with the hypocrisy, the secrets and the repressed emotions of bourgeois characters, which eventually explode into physical violence. Infidelity, guilt and murder in different combinations are the staple themes in his production. Alfred Hitchcock, whom Chabrol had interviewed and written a short book about in the 1950s, was a major influence on his work, as was Fritz Lang. Psychoanalysis was another: for the writing of one of his movies, *La Cérémonie* (1995), Chabrol had collaborated with a psychoanalyst because, he said, "It's very hard, when you deal with characters, not to use the Freudian grid, because the Freudian grid is composed of signs that also apply to the cinema" (in Feinstein 1996, p. 86).

In his seminal text, *Beyond the Pleasure Principle* (1920a), Freud had introduced the notion of a death drive (thanatos) coexisting with a life-affirming one (eros). This controversial hypothesis suggested that all organic matter (*homo sapiens* included) feels a somewhat obscure, regressive attraction to its inorganic sources. This idea was at least in part based on Freud's observation of a universal tendency to repeat traumatic events, such as those experienced by so many soldiers fighting in the bloody First World War (which had then just ended).

Focusing now on Chabrol's *Le Boucher*[23] I would suggest that Popaul (Jean Yanne), its protagonist, is also repeating early traumata of which he may have been the victim (he describes his father as abusive) by becoming himself a perpetrator of more traumata: not an unusual outcome, as we know from our clinical work, resulting from a process of identification with the aggressor. Thus Popaul becomes a butcher of animals (like his father) and then, by joining the French army and staying in it for fifteen years, the traumatized witness of the butchering committed by others. From the abattoir we go to the killing fields of Algeria and Indochina, and back again.

That the two activities, as a butcher and a soldier, overlap in his mind and may serve similar psychological purposes should not surprise us. We find several references in Popaul's speeches suggesting that for him people are not very different from animals. He calls his own father "a rat" and "'a swine," deems his teacher Mademoiselle Vachin "a cow by name and a cow by nature," and explains how the blood of animals (to be butchered, carved and then eaten) smells the same as that of human beings, who implicitly deserve a similar treatment. The first words Popaul utters during the wedding meal that opens the film, with reference to the joint of beef he prepares to carve, are: "I killed it myself. If it's no good, I'll cut my tongue out." Not to mention that, because of his senseless murders of women, as we gradually find out, he himself would be described (at least in tabloid-press language) as a beast.

We the viewers join him at a time when, having gone back to his father's job in the village, the destructive power of thanatos gets perversely mixed up in his mind with what we presume to be his immature understanding of eros. Hélène (Stéphane Audran), the head teacher in the local primary school, has had a good experience of love, even though she is still bearing the pain of a relationship unhappily ended in the past. This past love leaves her unwilling to take more risks with men. In contrast, we know nothing about Popaul's previous erotic experiences. What we are shown instead are his somewhat clumsy attempts to seduce Hélène by offering her meat (wrapped up as if it were a bunch of flowers) and cherries in brandy, and by volunteering to decorate her flat. We also become aware, as the narrative unfolds, that, alternating with such kind gestures towards a woman, Popaul is committing gruesome murders of other women. Who are they? Why does he kill them? How does he choose them? We are only told of the identity of one of them, the newlywed wife of Hélène's colleague, towards whom Popaul may have felt jealous. And his weapon, of course, could only be a carving knife. It is this perverse confusion of eros and thanatos, passion and murder, which has such a powerful, if understated, psychological representation in *Le Boucher.* Such a theme is a characteristic of much of Chabrol's cinematic production, but the twist in the tale this time is that the murderer eventually turns his carving knife against himself. The victim who had spent his life as a perpetrator has become a victim again, sacrificing himself like an unlikely lamb (or beef) on the altar of his love for a woman.

What part does Hélène play in the story? Not, we can be certain, that of the innocent (potential) victim of a sadistic murderer, but rather the role of a subtle accomplice, if only through her ambiguous affective involvement with him. Her seductive invitation to dinner and her birthday present (neither of which Popaul expected) combine with her clear message to him that she is not sexually available. He respects her wish, but then . . . he had not raped the three (or more) girls he had murdered either, something which had left even the police inspector surprised.

Figure 5.3 Jean Yanne and Stéphane Audran in *Le Boucher* (Chabrol 1970)

Not everything about Hélène is as straightforward as it appears: why is she acting seductively towards Popaul if she has already decided not to get more involved? Why does she hide his lighter in a drawer and lie to the police about not having found any clues to one of the murders? We are told that Hélène has given up on men, or at least on getting sexually involved with them, since her disappointment in a relationship suddenly terminated ten years earlier. "Never to make love can drive you crazy," says Popaul. "Making love can send you mad, too," answers Hélène. In her mind, she has replaced a love life with a successful professional one as a headmistress, and has replaced men with young pupils. We watch her reading to the children a passage from Honoré de Balzac, and taking them on two school trips: to the woods picking mushrooms (when she offers Popaul a lighter as a birthday present), and to the Lascaux caves (where he loses it).

What we do know is that Popaul and Hélène get together (whatever that ambiguous expression may mean). Their unconsummated relationship begins with their walk through the village after leaving the wedding party, a true tour-de-force long shot (three minutes and forty-six seconds) from Chabrol's camera. The unconscious magnet between them is that the man may be feeling attracted to her fascination with his own familiarity with cruelty, and the woman is somewhat perversely drawn towards it. This may ultimately be what saves her life.

In *Le Boucher* the platonic nature of the friendship developing between Hélène and Popaul could be construed as fuelling the outburst of his psychopathic tendencies, hitherto sublimated through the socially acceptable professional roles adopted by him: as a butcher and as an army man. It is indeed a feature of many psychopathic characters to present a pleasant, even charming façade, while they are prepared to commit the most heinous crimes, often without experiencing, consciously at least, any remorse.[24] Such a contrast is echoed in the film by that between its visuals and its sounds: between its setting, the apparently peaceful village of Trémolat in Dordogne, and the atmosphere conveyed by Pierre Jansen's music score, which warns us from the very first frames that something disturbing is brewing under the surface.

Popaul, like the psychopathic protagonist of *Jagged Edge* (Marquand 1985), a Hollywood film on a similar subject, fits this description well. He is kind and generous to Hélène, helpful whenever needed (whether to carve the roast for the guests at the wedding lunch, or to collect the children's exercise-books in her classroom). Even his pleasant physical appearance and demeanour, unlike that of many villains in films and in the popular imagination, does not make us suspicious about his tormented inner world. (I once heard a police officer comment that if criminals looked any different from you and me he would find his job too easy).

When Hélène, after several twists in the plot, becomes certain of Popaul's murderous guilt, she barricades herself in her school. But Popaul, a man with no respect for boundaries (he has been stalking her, watching her from the school-yard, going in and out at will from her classroom and her home, opening her drawers and cooking in her kitchen as if it was his own), still finds his way in. When she, and we the viewers, think that he is going to kill her, Hélène shuts her eyes, her face taking on an expression that suggests a mixture of fear of getting stabbed and a desire to be penetrated. The screen twice fades to black for brief moments. When the light returns, we, along with Hélène, realize that Popaul has stabbed himself to death, not her. He will die in the no-man's-land of a hospital lift, after a long car journey in the course of which he reveals his love to her, while his blood (and her tears) flow out from their bodies.

While neither sex or murder actually take place on the screen in the course of this "subtle, compassionate study of sexual frustration" (Bergan 2010), the struggle between eros and thanatos, these two intertwined "Heavenly Powers" as Freud calls them (1930, p. 145), is present throughout the film. The question as to which of the two ultimately prevails must remain unanswered.

*****

From the doomed lovers in Shakespeare's *Romeo and Juliet* to the *Liebestod* of Wagner's *Tristan und Isolde,* the association of eros with thanatos has been for centuries a *topos* of much drama, melodrama and literature in Western culture – not to mention cinema. Such an association between these two vast domains of human experience lends itself well to psychoanalytical interpretations. The combination of love and aggression always to be found in the Oedipal stage of development; the notion of the coexistence of libidinal and death drives, also applied to the vicissitudes of civilization; the realization of the fluidity of the boundaries between normality and perversion, with special reference to sadomasochism; the suggestion that the romantic fantasy of eternal love may be but our defensive attempt to deny the reality of our own mortality – these are some of the ideas informing our understanding of this association, troublesome but frequently met in the fictional world of cinema as indeed in real life too.

Pedro Almodóvar's fifth feature *Matador*[25] is an effective representation of the eros-and-thanatos configuration. One of that film's protagonists, former bullfighter Diego Montes (Nacho Martinez), has years before survived a serious accident in the ring (like the *matadora* in Almodóvar's *Talk to Her* 2002), and now walks Oedipus-like with a limp. Addicted to the slasher-horror-porn genre of videos, Diego has replaced the killing of bulls in the Plaza de Toros with the killing of female bullfighters in the bedroom. His counterpart and nemesis, criminal lawyer Maria Cardenal (Assumpta Serna), indulges in analogous murderous activities with her male lovers, penetrating their necks with a long hairpin as if it were a *banderilla* in order to satisfy her orgasmic desires.

It is inevitable that sooner or later such well-matched individuals should come across each other. "You and I are alike," says Diego to Maria when they meet on a bridge often used by people with suicidal intentions, "we're both obsessed with death." Their deadly erotic vicissitudes mirror those of an old film which we watch them watch together: the dramatic scene in King Vidor's *Duel in the Sun* (1946) when Gregory Peck and Jennifer Jones first shoot at each other, and then die in each other's arms.

Figure 5.4 Matador (Almodóvar 1986)

Probably present in everybody's conscious or unconscious normal fantasy life, the aforementioned association of eros and thanatos takes on pathological qualities whenever it makes lovers idealize death, or even actively pursue it. The meaning of the marriage vows phrase "Till death do us part" is then negated in the belief that death will not part the lovers at all. On the contrary, death will join them together for eternity as they engage in the destructive and self-destructive fantasy of a symbiotic union. Its regressive quality, rooted as it is in the earliest infantile experience of fusion with the primary object, is unmistakable.

I have so far been using the expression "eros *and* thanatos." However, it would be helpful to consider separately the different aspects of such a partnership. Sometimes eros must be treated as the *cause* of thanatos: an abandoned or betrayed lover (out of despair, need for revenge, or both) may turn to suicide, murder, or both. Such crimes of passion, especially if allegedly committed in order to defend the honour of the family, are encouraged within certain societies and even tolerated by their laws. Eros, however, could also get identified, or perhaps confused, with thanatos through a process involving what psychoanalysts conceptualize as the death drive. In its most extreme version, such an overidentification could lead to a pact between lovers, culminating in the *folie-à-deux* of double suicides (or are they not double homicides?) of the kind that in Almodóvar's film concludes Diego and Maria's erotic odyssey off-screen.

For the protagonists of *Matador* the wish to experience dying together during a passionate encounter is the tragic alternative to that of reaching together sexual climax.[26] But such an ultimate erotic activity can only be delusional, having as its purpose the avoidance of reality; for, once both lovers have passed away and their love is buried six feet under with them, there can be no second thoughts about the sincerity or intensity of their relationship, no future for it, and no threat to it from either inner or external sources.

Another instance of the unhealthy association of eros and thanatos can be found in necrophilia, consisting of the performance of sexual activities with corpses, a form of perversion we have already come across in Buñuel's *Belle-de-Jour* (see Chapter Two). In *Matador* Diego comes near to it when he asks his girlfriend Eva to close her eyes and play dead while he makes love to her (a less extreme arrangement than actually killing her). This is a situation comparable to the one Almodóvar himself would present fifteen years later in *Talk to Her* (2002) in which a male nurse makes love to a woman while she is in a state of deep coma.[27]

With references to themes also frequent in Buñuel's films, such as the consequences of the *mala educación* of a strict religious upbringing on the guilt-ridden, not-so-innocent, psychotic, virgin and telepathic character of Angel, and with a Buñuelian taste for a surrealistic outlook on the world, *Matador* also touches on the theme of fetishism, a deviant activity practiced by Maria who secretly collects bullfighting memorabilia. "Feminine fetishization," comments film scholar Paul Julian Smith, "points to the fragility of sexual difference" (Smith 2000, p. 70). Fetishism, though, is mostly present in *Matador* in a more subtle form, through a constant display of (and discourse about) outlandish costumes. Such a display culminates in the frantic, farcical fashion show filmed in a disused but apparently still blood-smelling slaughterhouse (like the one notable for its absence in Chabrol's *Le Boucher*), masterminded by Maestro Almodóvar himself. Don Pedro plays here the cameo role of a man too busy to answer a journalist's questions about the envy and intolerance of a divided Spain, while his own brother, and later producer, Agustin Almodóvar, is relegated to playing the secondary role of the second policeman.

Matador's impressive screenplay provides Almodóvar with a rich arena (or bullring) in which to show off his remarkable cinematic skills. The result is an unclassifiable, flamboyant pastiche of a story, suspended on a tightrope between transgressive eroticism, hilarious comedy, camp melodrama and old-fashioned romance. Its countless excesses, which may disturb some viewers, are in fact contained here within an impeccably designed scenography, elegant mise-en-scène and intelligent dialogues.

Okay, the metaphor of the corrida as sexual intercourse (or is it the other way round: sexual intercourse as a metaphor for the corrida?) may be a little trite. As a critic put it, "a doctorate in semiology isn't required to decipher the connection being made here" (Hinson 1988). But then we suspect Almodóvar is too sophisticated a filmmaker to have ever intended to lecture us on the symbolic significance of such an embedded, if now also contested, manifestation of Spanish folklore. He is just gently pulling our legs here, and we can allow ourselves to enjoy every minute of it.

****

Alfred Hitchcock's *Vertigo*[28] is by many considered his masterpiece: a movie "of uncanny maturity and insight, and if its characters are flawed, that is after all, only a measure of their patent humanity, and of the film's unsentimental yet profound passion" (Spoto 1976, p. 337).

Its plot can be summarized as follows: Scottie (James Stewart), a former police officer affected by phobic attacks of vertigo, lets his friend Gavin convince him to protect the beautifully mysterious Madeleine (Kim Novak), described to him as neurotic, by following her around San Francisco. This however turns out to be part of a hoax intended to get Scottie to witness her suicidal jump from a bell tower, while in fact the woman falling is Gavin's murdered wife. When some time later Scottie meets a Judy Barton who resembles Madeleine, he falls in love with her without realizing that she is the same woman he thought he had seen kill herself. As he becomes suspicious and forces Judy to go back to the bell tower in an attempt to make her confess her complicity with Gavin, she accidentally trips to her death.

An original and convincing interpretation of this film along psychoanalytic lines suggests that Scottie, not unlike some of the characters we have met in *Cabiria* and in *Amores Perros,* lives out the rescue fantasy, in identification with the Greek mythological character of Orpheus, of striving to bring his Eurydice, the woman he is supposed to be shadowing, back from the Underworld. Another interpretation is that Scottie transforms himself into a Knight (he had been a policeman) determined to kill a mysterious Dragon endangering Beauty, until eventually "the valiant Knight turns out to be as helpless and lonely as his Beauty, and in the final scene as ruthless and lethal as the Dragon" (Berman 1997).

My suggestion is that *Vertigo* is built around a profound unconscious internal conflict that is most evident in Scottie but also in his complementary object Madeleine/Judy. The idea of internal conflict between opposites in mental life is crucial to a psychoanalytic understanding of all psychological phenomena, both normal and pathological, seen as compromise formations between two contrasting emotional needs. Since the clinical observation of Little Hans (Freud 1909) this is well known in the case of all phobias and, in the instance which concerns us here, of acrophobia, the fear of heights. As the title of a psychoanalytic book on the subject suggests (*Emotional Vertigo: Between Anxiety and Pleasure* [Quinodoz 1994]), those who suffer from this psychological condition feel as attracted as they feel terrified of falling into the void. In their experience, horror and excitement, fear and desire are but two sides of the same coin.

Relevant to our reading of Hitchcock's film is a specific application of the idea of internal conflict to the dynamics of sexual deviations. Analysts working with patients diagnosed as sexually perverse often come across their constant fascination, and at the same time dread, for a sort of black hole associated in their unconscious minds with a powerful pulling back towards the mother's body – a predicament Glasser (1986) calls "Core Complex." The perverse activity is understood as a solution to the dilemma faced by those individuals who feel a tragic fascination for regressive dependence towards an engulfing object, which may be both protective and destructive. They cannot separate from the object nor let themselves be swallowed by it, though they try to achieve both things at the same time.

We can then try to interpret Scottie's psychology as being dominated by an internal conflict consisting of a vertiginous attraction for something which, at the same time, is also experienced as dangerously entrapping and deadly. Madeleine is presented as a dream: "The fascination she exerts is the fascination of death, a drawing toward oblivion and final release; the yearning for the dream . . . become[s] logically a yearning for death" (Wood 1989, p. 114). But Scottie's attraction for Madeleine is flawed from the beginning. Throughout his relationship with her he is deluded (not without her connivance) into becoming a sort of psychoanalyst, helping her to recover her lost memories, to interpret her dreams, to free her from her obsession with a static portrait in the San Francisco art gallery and to integrate the different aspects of her split personality. In reality, though, it is not her he is desperate to cure, but himself: his phobias, his vertigo, his guilt. And in the end he will succeed but, paradoxically, not through winning her love, but through losing her forever.

As a result of this intrinsic confusion we, the spectators, are left dangling in the void, so to speak, suspended between opposite poles, unable to form an unambiguous identification with the main characters, but constantly oscillating backwards and forwards, and to be left with a sense of anxious excitement. This suspension is precisely what makes *Vertigo* such a balanced masterpiece. For instance, we are intrigued and disturbed by the concrete evidence of the passing of centuries on the cross-section of the evergreen *Sequoia Semperviva* that is admired by our heroes during a trip to a National Park; we are tempted for a moment by the most improbable of paranormal explanations, instead of the more rational clinical one, for Madeleine's identity confusion in front of the portrait of a dead woman uncannily resembling her; we dive with Scottie into the cold waters of the San Francisco Bay in order to live out his powerful rescue fantasy; the spiraling staircase on which Scottie tries to follow the apparently suicidal Madeleine captivates us and then, as stairwell, traumatizes us like the rooftops had done in the opening scene of the film; we are, or think we are, witnesses to suicidal, homicidal and even accidental drops from the top of the San Juan Baptista church tower; we are seduced, with Scottie – whom Martin Scorsese described as "a hero driven purely by obsession" (Scorsese 1999) – by the obscure and unreachable object of his desire in the shape of Madeleine's body.

About two-thirds of the way through *Vertigo*, Hitchcock breaks with the suspense-thriller genre tradition (but remains consistent with his own narrative style; see Chapter One). He gives his spectators an unexpected quick flashback: a most dramatic (and implausible) sequence of his friend Gavin throwing his real wife's body from the top of the bell tower. In this way Hitchcock involves his spectators in finding out the truth, or at least a crucial fragment of it, about Madeleine/Judy before Scottie does. This throws us into a state of anxiety: after experiencing directly Scottie's shock at what we believed to be Madeleine's suicide, "now we experience a further, and worse shock: not only is she dead – she never existed. . . . The revelation cuts the ground away from under our feet, and makes us painfully aware of the degree of our previous involvement in what is now proved to be a cheap hoax" (Wood 1989, p. 121).

This scene echoes the initial one (with Scottie dangling from the gutter on the rooftop) in that they both involve traumas for the spectator. Hitchcock's disclosure forces us to abandon (prematurely? timely?) our previous position of naive childhood beliefs and to assume the role of knowledgeable, responsible and perhaps also cynical adults who can no longer pretend to ignore the facts of life. The episode where we are shown an aspect of reality whose existence we had ignored does not just mean that now "we are finally allowed to be the insightful analysts, the successful detectives," as Berman (1997, p. 977) puts it. Rather, the episode can be read as a metaphor for all the big and small traumas, exciting as they are frightening, which from the Primal Scene onwards are part and parcel of growing up, of finding out the truth (or at least some truths) about human relationships and of gradually moving towards independence. But this is disturbing, as is the case whenever we discover an important secret while we would have felt more comfortable to remain in a state of blissful ignorance. That little girls don't have little willies. That parents have sexual intercourse. That our cousin is not really our uncle's child. That we are not immortal. Not to mention, of course, the controversial existence of Father Christmas. We undergo a journey of discoveries, and of further concealments, that lasts throughout our lives.

Scottie now is left behind us, still as blind to the meaning of what occurs around him as Oedipus was, though a sense of impending doom is beginning to emerge as he proceeds with his frantic need to retransform Judy into the woman of his desires. When Judy resurrects, dressed and made up and hairstyled and bejewelled as Madeleine (but hers is only the stuff dreams or films are made of), we are given "a breathtaking moment of romantic fantasy fulfillment; Scottie feels he has succeeded in defying death, in bringing Eurydice back from Hades" (Berman 1997, p. 978).

Figure 5.5 Kim Novak and James Stewart in *Vertigo* (Hitchcock 1958)

The truth, though, is that it is not Scottie transforming Judy into Madeleine, but rather she turning Scottie, out of her love for him, into a sort of voyeuristic and fetishistic pervert – a case of Core Complex suitable, perhaps, for psychoanalytic intervention. Furthermore, from the moment Hitchcock takes us behind Scottie's back to show us the missing piece in the jigsaw puzzle, our identification with him, with his salvage fantasy and with his romantic quest, becomes problematic. Our attention is shifted away from the object of his search and we become curious instead about whether and how and when he will find out what we, the viewers, already know.

The Master of Suspense is here also trying to tell us something important about cinema itself: its box of tricks, its capacity to present a façade as if it were a building, a model train as if it were a full size one, day-for-night. Four years earlier, his movie *Rear Window,* as we shall see in the next chapter, was his statement about cinema as a voyeuristic exercise that manipulates us into seeing only what it wants us to see. Here in *Vertigo* Hitchcock-the-Magician, with the extraordinary timing of this dénouement scene, takes us by the hand backstage to the Paramount Studios and forces us to confront the cinema's ultimate function (one that is in stark contrast with that of psychoanalysis): to give us fictional fantasies in the shape of reality. Nothing more, perhaps, than flickering lights and shadows, and twinkling stars.

Notes

1. Two more specific aspects of the general theme of how love is portrayed in movies are dealt with in more detail in other parts of the book: prostitution in Chapter Two and voyeurism in Chapter Six.
2. Romance was "formerly a long narrative in verse or prose, originally written in one of the Romance dialects (those derived from low Latin: Portuguese, Spanish, Catalan, Provençal, French, Italian and Romanian) about the adventures of knights and other chivalric heroes. Later, a fictitious tale of wonderful and extraordinary events characterized by much imagination and idealization, with an emphasis on excitement, love and adventure" (from *Webster's Dictionary, College Edition,* 1966).
3. *Ossessione* (Italy 1943). Directed by Luchino Visconti. Written by Luchino Visconti, Mario Alicata et al., from James M. Cain's novel *The Postman Always Rings Twice.* Starring Clara Calamai (Giovanna Bragana) and Massimo Girotti (Gino Costa).
4. It was in relation to *Ossessione* that the label *Neorealismo* was used for the first time. Its editor, Mario Serandrei, wrote to Visconti: "I wouldn't know how to define this kind of movie-making other than by calling it 'neo-realistic.'" More details about Italian Neorealism can be found in Chapter Three.
5. *A Pornographic Affair [Une Liaison pornographique]* (France and Belgium 1999). Directed by Frédéric Fonteyne. Written by Philippe Blasband. Starring Nathalie Baye (Elle) and Sergi Lòpez (Lui).
6. To mention just a few from those years: Michelle Delville's *La Lectrice* (1988), Patrice Leconte's *The Hairdresser's Husband* (1990) and Claude Sautet's *Un Coeur en Hiver* (1991).
7. The Greek words *porneia* and *grafikos* mean, respectively, "prostitution or lewd acts" and "graphic." "Pornographic" is therefore the representation of something obscene, not the obscene thing itself. The adjective *pornographic* could therefore be applied only to such things as images and texts (say in a play, a song, a novel, a film), but not to an affair.

8. A direct reference to Plato's Myth of the Cave in a film can be found in Bernardo Bertolucci's *The Conformist* (1970).
9. The fantasy of immortality is related to unconscious timelessness and to the infantile undifferentiated temporal dimension of the omnipresent (Sabbadini 1989).
10. For psychoanalytic review articles on the theme of rescue fantasies, see Esman (1987) and Gillman (1992).
11. *Amores Perros* (Mexico 2000). Directed, produced and coedited by Alejandro Gonzáles Iñárritu. Written by Guillermo Arriaga. Starring Gael García Bernal (Octavio), Emilio Echevarria (El Chivo), Vanessa Bauche (Susana), Goya Toledo (Valeria).
12. Such a narrative device, also exploited in disaster movies, had famously been used in Thornton Wilder's novel *The Bridge of San Luis Rey* (1927). It begins thus: "On Friday noon, July the twentieth, 1714, the finest bridge in all Peru broke and precipitated five travelers into the gulf below" (Part One, "Perhaps an Accident," p. 1), and proceeds to analyze their characters and explore their relationships to each other. Wilder's constant preoccupation with rescue fantasies, which Glenn (1986) attributes to his being the surviving member of a pair of premature twins, is relevant to the theme of the present chapter.
13. This motif is often found in fairy tales, from Little Red Riding Hood, Rapunzel and Sleeping Beauty to George Bernard Shaw's *Pygmalion* (1913); in collective regressive fantasies of a nostalgic Golden Age (Ovid's *Aurea Aetas*); in the religions promoting hope in a Messiah still to come to earth (for the Jews) or already arrived to sacrifice his own life for mankind on the cross (for the Christians), or the belief in reincarnation (for the Hindus); and, of course, in countless works of fiction, be they novels, plays, operas, soaps or films. These last ones include Westerns, war movies, melodramas and such popular blockbusters as *Schindler's List* (Spielberg 1993) and *Titanic* (Cameron 1997).
14. Classical Greek mythology has provided psychoanalysis with some of its fundamental narratives. Sophocles' dramatization of the story of Oedipus has in its multifaceted ramifications thrown an all-important light on the developmental history of human individuals, their conscious and unconscious internal worlds, and their interpersonal relationships. Other Greek myths, such as those of Narcissus or of Electra, have also helped us to clarify many normal and pathological mental phenomena. Elsewhere I have referred to the Homeric legend of Odysseus's encounter with the Sirens in relation to the technical problems involved in countertransferential erotic attraction (Sabbadini 1993) and to the story of Icarus's suicidal flight to explain manic episodes as instances of defenses in the face of separation anxiety (Sabbadini 1999).
15. The myth of Orpheus continues with his renunciation of women (in one version, turning to homosexuality) which provokes a band of angry Maenads to tear him apart. His head and lyre, still singing, float down the Hebrus river to the island of Lesbos, where Apollo will protect Orpheus's head from a snake and endow it with prophetic powers; hence his status for the ancients as "not only the archetypal poet but also the founder of a mystical religion known as Orphism" (Segal 1989, p. 1). Part of the everlasting attraction of this myth depends on the personality of its protagonist, Orpheus, being not just a great poet and musician, but someone who would use his art to tame wild animals, to move plants and stones, and to get dolphins to emerge from the sea to listen and enjoy his songs. This in itself gives him an almost godlike quality, placing him above other mortals, in a fantasy space where others would feel induced to identify with, idealize and envy him.
16. Limentani (1989) describes certain psychoanalytic patients who, in identification with Orpheus's ambivalence, are unable to repair the Oedipal situation.
17. The myth of Orpheus and Eurydice has fascinated artists, writers and composers who, also in identification with its protagonist, have then reproduced it in their works. I shall limit myself in this context to mention Rainer Maria Rilke's fifty-five *Sonnets*

to Orpheus (1922) and Christoph W. Gluck's opera *Orfeo e Euridice* (1762) where, the gods having promptly forgiven Orpheus for his voyeuristic peccadillo, the tragic ending of the story is replaced by an improbable "and they lived happily thereafter." Not surprisingly, this classical myth has also inspired filmmakers: explicitly so in two classic modern adaptations of it, Jean Cocteau's *Orphée* (1950) and Marcel Camus's *Orfeu Negro (Black Orpheus)* (1959) as well as, more indirectly, in such masterpieces as Alfred Hitchcock's *Vertigo* (1958), where an apparently deceased woman comes back to life only to then die for the second time (see this chapter); and Bernardo Bertolucci's *Ultimo Tango a Parigi (Last Tango in Paris)* (1972) where, as Kline (1976) has acutely observed, the protagonist's passionate affair with his lover, following his wife's death by suicide, shares many features with the original Greek story.

18. One is reminded here of Paolo and Francesca, the famous lovers Dante places among the damned because of their adulterous relationship. Paolo was the brother of Francesca's husband Gianciotto. Also, in Shakespeare's *Hamlet*, Gertrude marries her brother-in-law, who had killed her first husband, Claudius.

19. These scenes, with their extreme brutality, are reminiscent of those in Michael Cimino's *The Deer Hunter* (1978), where drug addicts play Russian roulette in a sordid Vietnamese den, surrounded by an excited crowd of punters betting on their survival.

20. She reminds us of James Stewart, with his leg stuck in a plaster cast throughout Hitchcock's *Rear Window* (1954) (see Chapter Six), and of one-legged Catherine Deneuve in Buñuel's *Tristana* (1970).

21. The adjective *cynical* derives from the Greek *kunikos*, which translates as "dog-like."

22. By observing the emotional tension between this bearded man's wish for revenge on the one hand and the need to control his destructive feelings on the other, one is reminded of a similarly dignified negotiation of conflict in another bearded father-figure, Moses, as described by Freud (1914). According to him, Moses, angry at his people for worshiping the Golden Calf, first "desired to act, to spring up and take vengeance and forget the Tables; but he has overcome the temptation, and he will now remain seated and still in his frozen wrath [. . .] He remembered his mission and for its sake renounced an indulgence of his feelings" (1914, pp. 229–230). Freud's brilliant if somewhat unconvincing interpretation of the meaning of Michelangelo's statue of the Jewish leader may be explained as compensation for the powerful emotions Freud had felt himself as a child when his father had told him that, many years earlier, an anti-Semitic thug had insulted him and thrown his fur cap into the mud. Jacob Freud had responded to the provocation by simply picking up his cap and walking away. "This struck me," wrote Freud (1900, p. 197), "as unheroic conduct on the part of the big, strong man who was holding the little boy by the hand."

23. *Le Boucher* (France 1970). Directed and written by Claude Chabrol. Starring Stéphane Audran (Hélène) and Jean Yanne (Popaul).

24. Such as the lead character in Michael Powell's *Peeping Tom* (see Chapter Six).

25. *Matador* (Spain 1986). Directed by Pedro Almodóvar. Written by Pedro Almodóvar, Jesus Ferreo et al. Starring Nacho Martinez (Diego Montes), Assumpta Serna (Maria Cardenal), Antonio Banderas (Angel), and Carmen Maura (Julia).

26. It is not a coincidence that orgasm is sometimes referred to as *la petite mort* (small death).

27. See Sabbadini (2006).

28. *Vertigo* (United States 1958). Directed by Alfred Hitchcock. Written by Alec Coppel, Samuel Taylor et al. Starring James Stewart (Scottie), Kim Novak (Madeleine/Judy), and Barbara Bel Geddes (Midge).

Chapter 6

Watching voyeurs

Films on scopophilia

Looking and being looked at play an important part in the establishment and maintenance of interpersonal relationships. Should we then come to the rather extreme conclusion that we are all potential voyeurs? While this would be an unnecessary generalization, we could also reasonably claim that, on account of our polymorphously perverse infancy, it is a commonplace. We psychoanalysts, moreover, make ourselves especially vulnerable to being labeled as voyeurs (though of the auditory rather than the visual kind), insofar as our profession involves a curiosity for, or even a probing into, our analysands' internal worlds, including their darkest fantasies and secret passions.

If we now narrow down our field of vision and focus it on the specific sense in which we could describe ourselves as voyeurs in our capacity as cinemagoers, or should we say as film-lovers, we realize that when the films in question are *about* voyeurism itself, as are those to be discussed in this chapter, we find ourselves faced with an intriguing situation. What we would be describing is no longer just the indulgent voyeuristic activity of watching a film, with all the desire, anticipation, pleasure or disappointment that such an activity involves. What we, the spectators of these films, would be doing is *watching other voyeurs like ourselves.* In other words, our identifications on the one hand and our visual excitement on the other will have as their objects not only the film itself, but also the subjects and objects of the voyeuristic activities projected on the screen – a screen thus turning into the disturbing, distorting mirror of our own suppressed desires.

Christian Metz's classic essay *The Imaginary Signifier* (1974) is in this respect an enlightening text. Answering his own question about where we can locate a film spectator's point of view, Metz argues that all a viewer can do is to identify with the camera which has looked before him. But of course in the cinema there is no camera, only its "representative consisting of another apparatus, called precisely a 'projector.' . . . During the performance the spectator is the searchlight . . . duplicating the projector, which itself duplicates the camera, and he is also the sensitive surface duplicating the screen, which itself duplicates the film-strip" (Metz 1974, pp. 49–51). All of which applies to how movies were being shot and shown back in the distant 1970s before digital cinema started to replace the film camera with its own new apparatuses.

What Metz goes on to say, though, still applies today: the voyeur "is very careful to maintain a gulf, an empty space between the object and the eye, the object and his own body: his look fastens the object at the right distance" (Metz 1974, p. 60). The desire, as we learn from Lacan, consists in an attempt, inevitably doomed to failure, to fill a void, while leaving it gaping so that the desire can survive *qua* desire. In the end the desire has no object, or rather it pursues an imaginary one to be kept at a safe distance, for it would otherwise threaten to overwhelm its subject. What is peculiar about cinema is that not only does it allow us to perceive our object from a distance (through the senses of sight and hearing) but also, as we have noticed earlier, "what remains in that distance is now no longer the object itself, it is a delegate" (Metz 1974, p. 61). We have then a perverse situation whereby while "the actor was present when the spectator was not [during the shooting of the film], the spectator is present when the actor is no longer [during its projection]: a failure to meet of the voyeur and the exhibitionist" (Metz 1974, p. 63).

Freud observed that in its preliminary stage the scopophilic drive is autoerotic, and that "it has indeed an object, but that object is part of the subject's own body" (Freud 1915, p. 130). This situation is the source of both voyeurism and exhibitionism. Remembering this, we can identify two contrasting perspectives on the relationship between films and their spectators, perspectives which correspond to two different kinds of voyeurism. From the first perspective, films could be considered as exhibitionistic objects, since being watched is for them (not unlike for actors on the stage) the purpose itself of their existence, in a context where the voyeurs' satisfaction depends on their object's wish to be watched. From the second perspective, though, films are not exhibitionistic objects at all, for they do not watch us watching them: the voyeurs' satisfaction depends on the fact that the object they are watching (i.e. the film) is unaware, so to speak, of being watched.

At this point we need to differentiate two complementary kinds of voyeurism. I shall call them *covert* and *collusive*, respectively. Covert voyeurism is a narcissistic form of penetrative aggression directly related to Primal Scene fantasies. It involves gratification through the watching of objects who are themselves unaware of being watched (the furtive activity, to give an example, of a peeping Tom hiding in a girls' changing room). Collusive voyeurism on the other hand involves the experience of pleasure through the activity of watching objects who are well aware that they are being watched (for instance, strippers in a nightclub). This is a more sophisticated form of perversion because it implies some recognition that others are not just extensions of one's own self, but real persons responding to the voyeuristic activities of the subject and potentially getting exhibitionistic satisfaction from being looked at. Both these situations, with countless variations on the theme, present themselves in real life, as well as in films on the theme of voyeurism.

These films, such as those we will examine in this chapter, give the medium of cinema an opportunity for self-reflection by performing the cultural function of representing conflictual aspects of our inner reality and object relationships. In its capacity as a social provider of visual and auditory messages which, not unlike psychoanalysis itself, can confirm our Weltanschauung or challenge it at its very roots, cinema will be acknowledging its responsibilities towards its spectators. Specifically in the emotionally loaded areas of sexual experience, identity and behaviour, and of the constantly shifting boundaries between normality and pathology, both psychoanalysis and cinema are powerful languages that allow us – or sometimes even force us – to reconsider our assumptions, values and beliefs about ourselves.

*****

Having already looked at Hitchcock's *Spellbound* and *Vertigo,* let us now consider another of his masterpieces: *Rear Window.*[1] Its main character is Jefferies (James Stewart), a photojournalist stuck in his apartment with a leg in a plaster. To fight boredom when he is not being visited by his beautiful girlfriend Lisa (Grace Kelly), he indulges in the covert voyeuristic activity of watching from his rear window what goes on in the apartments of the house opposite his (few windows seem to have had curtains in those days). His subjects include the antics of a young couple and the disappearance of a woman whose body was possibly cut into pieces and smuggled out in a suitcase. By the end, of course, all will be dramatically revealed.

On the surface, then, we are presented here with a mini-cliffhanger of a light comedy murder-story. At a more careful examination, however, Hitchcock's masterpiece turns out to be a most original multilayered objet d'art, the exhibitionistic target itself of intriguing scopophilic speculations. Let us consider a brief selection of the analytically inspired ones.

Figure 6.1 James Stewart in *Rear Window* (Hitchcock 1954)

Several authors (including Truffaut 1983) equate the Jimmy Stewart character with the spectator in the cinema. The screen is represented by the apartments across the courtyard: boxes of puppets whose frustrations can drive them to perversion, suicide and murder. All we can ever see are but projections of our own desires, in an attempt to work out our problems in fantasy form. Others will insist that *Rear Window* is a dream, not only because it could indeed be interpreted like one (for instance, we viewers are invited by its "manifest content" to construct a coherent narrative from fragments assembled through Primary Process mechanisms), but because its impact derives from the fact that the film itself, the story of which takes place between intervals of Jefferies' sleep, is structured and made to function like a dream (Benton 1984).

While some question the label of voyeurism in relation to Jefferies' behaviour on the grounds that his looking is motivated not by perverse sexual needs but by sheer boredom and curiosity (Sharff 1997), for others *Rear Window* "is essentially grounded on the coalescence of two convergent psychic mechanisms, an intense fear of object loss . . . and a sadistically interpreted primal scene" (Almansi 1992). Several authors emphasize that the film's protagonist is a man who has never come to terms with himself and can only escape from examining his own condition by spying on other people, for his gazing gives him a sense of power over those he watches, but without any accompanying responsibility (Wood 1989). It seems easier to Jefferies, I would add, to frame an uxoricide (a sort of doppelgänger on whom he can project his own *noir* fantasies) than to let his own fair (Mona) Lisa frame him into marriage. She, Grace Kelly, was soon to succeed in real life with a fairy-tale prince on the French Riviera.

We could not easily disagree with any of these interpretations. They are pertinent to Hitchcock's own text and subtext, logically coherent, aesthetically valid and enriching to our understanding of the film. All we can do is try and add our own jigsaw-puzzle piece to the overall picture. This metaphor happens to be appropriate, for *fragmentation* is the aspect of *Rear Window* I would like to concentrate on. In this respect Jefferies' fractured leg in a plaster cast (ambiguously both erect and impotent) is but the starting point of a series of further fragmentations which provide the backbone, so to speak, to the whole film. In his company we are seduced into focusing our eyes (or binoculars) on the multiple silent movies (more than one third of *Rear Window* is without dialogue), framed by windows, movies simultaneously projected onto the flats of a number of disturbingly over-normal neighbours: frustrated alcoholic artists, suicidal lonelyhearts, middle-aged couples with their displaced love on doomed *Dei ex machina* pets, and the we-can't-get-enough-of-it newlyweds hiding behind rolled-down blinds. Not to mention, of course, the unmentionable.

The fragmentations, both in content and form, of the main characters' identities, of the institution of marriage as society's supporting structure, of the architecture of the buildings (which reminds one of Mondrian's paintings) and indeed of the movie itself, plus the probable cutting into pieces of a physical female body, all contribute to our uncanny experience in front of the screen.

Gruesome stuff indeed, if Benton is right in suggesting that *Rear Window* "is a mystery about a mutilation: Did it occur? If so, how were the parts disposed of, by suitcase, trunk, or shovel? Which parts went where? . . . Mrs Thorwald's body – chopped into portable pieces – haunts the entire movie without ever being shown" (Benton 1984, p. 489). Hitchcock's frequent humorous touches are not enough to help us survive the onslaught. We also need a unifying element, and this we find in our almost total identification with Jefferies' point of view, paralyzed inside his claustrophobic room with a rear view, much as we are tied down ourselves to our cinema armchairs. With few remarkable exceptions, such as when we are allowed to watch Lars (L-A-R-S: even his name is fragmented into separate letters) Thorwald leave the house with a mysterious lady while Jefferies is asleep, we only see what Jefferies sees, only know what he knows. But this reassures us that at least we are not more psychotic, even if we are not less perverse, than he. To survive as viewers (and re-viewers) our interpretative task must involve a re-composition of the dissociated elements, a re-membering of the dis-membered fragments.

The film can also be seen as expressing, through the harsh words of Nurse Stella and old friend Doyle, a moral criticism of voyeurism as an invasion of privacy – a theme, by the way, that must have been prominent on Hollywood film-makers' agendas, or at least on their minds, during the McCarthy era when *Rear Window* was made. Even Lisa, who we can safely assume has never read *Three Essays on the Theory of Sexuality,* seems to know that the eyes are the voyeur's erotogenic zone (Freud 1905, p. 169) when she turns Jefferies' wheelchair away from the window, removes the binoculars out of his hand and tells him with diagnostic accuracy: "The way you look into people's windows is sick."

Yet, we may ask, what is Mr Hitchcock himself doing behind the camera that films Jimmy Stewart behind that phallic prosthetic eye of his telephoto lens? And aren't we watching *Rear Window,* protected by the darkness of a cinema, in the hope of having our own most primitive Oedipal curiosities (about sex, castration and murder) satisfied? As Hitchcock told Truffaut about Jefferies: "Sure, he's a snooper, but aren't we all?" (in Truffaut 1983, p. 216).

*****

Polish director Krzysztof Kieslowski acquired international success in 1988 with *The Decalogue,* ten one-hour-long films for television reflecting on contemporary moral dilemmas. He released the two most powerful episodes (numbers Five and Six) also separately in expanded feature-length versions: *A Short Film about Killing* (1988) and *A Short Film about Love* (1988).

The universal themes of loyalty, love, sincerity, faith, compassion and their opposites, which provide the background to Kieslowski's and his co-screen-playwright Krzysztof Piesiewicz's stories, all set in or around the same block of flats in the Warsaw of the 1980s, have only indirect relationships with the biblical injunctions of the Ten Commandments. While being independent or even critical of the precepts of any formal ideology (be it religious or political) they nevertheless represent a powerful statement about the risks of allowing our lives to be dominated by individual human passions without exercising ethical and social control over them – without, in other words, a sense of emotional responsibility. In this we can notice a similarity with the films of one of Kieslowski's mentors, Ingmar Bergman; though if you asked Kieslowski which directors have influenced him the most, he would probably reply Shakespeare, Dostoevsky and Kafka.

In *A Short Film about Love*[2] Kieslowski uses a rich tapestry of irony, humour and drama to weave his tale of interpersonal suffering, punctuated by Zbigniew Preisner's relentless yet delicate musical score. The Polish director delves with extraordinary sympathy into the hearts of his two main characters, Tomek (Olaf Lubaszenko) and Magda (Grazina Szapolowska), to examine the intricacies of their inner worlds. "There is more real feeling in this brief feature," as a critic wrote, "than in a hundred full-length Hollywood romantic comedies" (Berardinelli 1994). The great qualities of *A Short Film about Love* are its simplicity of structure, precision of camera work, incisiveness of dialogue, and sensitivity in its handling of the tension between eroticism and compassion. There is something so compelling and almost overwhelming about the humanity of this film, the accuracy with which it explores the emotional complexity of relationships and their often inevitable consequences, that one might feel tempted to just enjoy the experience without even attempting to analyze it.

However, in our effort to look further, and with the critical help of our psychoanalytic optical instruments, I suggest that we consider this film from the perspective of its search for an elusive meeting point, for a new interpersonal focus. Kieslowski's moral message clearly concerns the existential dangers of prying into other people's private spaces (with telescopes, binoculars, telephones), rupturing containers or crossing their boundaries (we watch Tomek shattering a window to burglar the school, forcing false notices into Magda's letter-box, slitting his own wrists), or indeed spilling out their contents (her milk, his semen and then blood, their tears).

These elements, central as they are to the film's narrative and iconology, are only the background to what I think is Kieslowski's deeper intention: representing the struggle of his two characters to find the optimal distance, or perhaps the optimal closeness, from one another. As they come from psychologically different places, even if they live in two identical blocks of flats facing each other, their needs are different. To oversimplify: Tomek searches for love without sex, Magda sex without love. And the point of convergence, somewhere in the trajectory of their lives, seems to be an illusory wish never to be realized. Here we can notice a parallel with the psychoanalytic situation, insofar as analysts and analysands are also in the position of having to constantly negotiate, adjust and readjust their relative distance, or perhaps proximity, to one another.[3]

Tomek, brought up in an orphanage and now living with the mother of an absent friend, is a shy nineteen-year-old with delinquent tendencies. We see him stealing a telescope which allows him to zoom in on Magda, the beautiful woman with a weaving hobby who has become the obsessional object of his desires. We know that he withholds her mail and sends her forged notices of payments (letting her be accused of trying to swindle the post office); that he lies about the presence of a gas leak in her apartment; that he hides her empty milk bottle and again lies to her about it. We also become aware of his self-destructive tendencies long before his attempt to bleed himself to death by slashing his wrists with a razor blade: he had already played the game of stabbing his hand with a pair of scissors and, after Magda's rejection, he had climbed on top of her building, most likely with suicidal intentions, where he had ended up sucking on a piece of ice, indicating perhaps both his experiences of deprivation as an abandoned child and his current need to make himself cooler in order to survive the harshness of human existence.

As someone having so little to offer others, it is ironic that Tomek should get jobs where he is given something to deliver: mail that, like his passion for learning foreign languages, represents his wish to communicate, and milk standing for his need for the mother's breast which he must have missed as an orphaned child and has only recently found in his landlady. It seems significant that it should be this wonderfully maternal woman, forced by circumstances to displace her affection for her own son onto Tomek, to be the one taking over from him the milk-delivery job after he ends up in hospital.

For Tomek, who has no experience of sexual closeness, the problem is how to approach Magda without letting her become either too intimate or too rejecting. His eyes, with a little prosthetic help from increasingly powerful optical instruments, let him travel the distance that separates her from himself and covertly penetrate her space with the same clumsy intrusiveness of the false notices he puts through her letter-box and of his wordless or apologetic telephone messages – his only available means of relating to her. Like a moth to a flame, he gets closer and closer until the warmth of his own passion nearly destroys him. Yet, as his

Figure 6.2 Olaf Lubaszenko in *A Short Film about Love* (Kieslowski 1988)

initial masturbatory interest for Magda as object of instinctual gratification is replaced by the love in which he does believe, she stops being for him just a body to watch and is gradually transformed by him into a real person. We see Tomek twice averting his eyes off the telescope at the very moments when Magda gets physically intimate with her boyfriends. Lovesickness overtakes voyeuristic excitement.

For Magda, only a little older than Tomek but much more experienced in the facts of life, the process is in many respects the opposite. Having had her wings burnt by love in the past (not unlike Hélène in *Le Boucher,* see Chapter Five), she is now trying to move away from it but is terrified of loneliness. She adopts a cynical attitude to relationships by becoming physically close to her objects (a stream of lovers who gain her the reputation of a rude acronym) while keeping emotionally distant from them.

"I am not good," she tells Tomek when he tries to give her a small present which she feels she does not deserve any more than his declared love. Magda's insecurity, her failure in relationships, her disappointment in the affairs of the heart are all powerfully expressed by her crying after spilling some milk and doing nothing to pick the bottle up – a scene which becomes a turning point in the story. Tomek, who cannot himself cry, is moved by her despair and finally finds the courage to talk to her about his true feelings. Unlike Tomek, who has dishonestly found out too much about her, Magda does not even know his name. But faced with his love – as genuine as it is perverted, as innocent as it is intrusive, passionate as it is immature – eventually she can no longer sustain her defensive use of her persona, body and all.

At this point Tomek and Magda appear to meet halfway through their journeys in opposite directions. But it is only an illusion, for as soon as the gap between them might be bridged, as soon as he accepts her seductive invitation to step through the threshold of her life, everything begins to collapse. When, at the dramatic climax of their encounter, she dismisses his feelings by telling him, "That's all there is to love" – a moment of premature shameful pleasure and a wet patch on his trousers – we know that she can be as cruel to herself as she is to him. Here a momentous shift occurs when our antihero, humiliated and hurt by her cynicism, runs from her apartment. We the viewers/voyeurs, having always glimpsed Magda's flat N° 376 from Tomek's and his telescope's perspective, are now left inside with Magda watching him go across the courtyard that separates their lives through *her* pair of binoculars, and sharing for the first time her point of view. His original covert voyeurism has become their joint collusive one. From now on the story of his love for her becomes the story of her love for him: the formal shift in perspective heralds and underscores the change in the narrative of their emotions. It is no longer Tomek pursuing her; it is Magda searching after him.

Kieslowski provided two different conclusions to the television and to the feature versions of this film. He describes the television ending to be closer to his view of how things really are in life, "dry, laconic and also very simple. Magda goes to the post office and Tomek tells her: 'I don't spy on you any more.' And we know that he really won't spy on her ever again and maybe he won't spy on anybody" (in Stok 1993, p. 170). In the feature film's ending, on the other hand, Magda uses Tomek's own telescope to watch herself in a flashback memory of her defining moment of despair in front of her existence's spilled chances. But now she imagines that Tomek, gently resting his hand on her shoulder, might redeem her with his love, like Alfredo had done for Violetta in *La Traviata*, that "Long Melodrama About Love."

In a sense, nothing is resolved, and how could it be? But perhaps, in the process, they and we have gained "an understanding of the great pain and fragility that can result from the simple act of opening one's heart" (Berardinelli 1994).

*****

Having watched an over-curious journalist snoop from his rear window in Hitchcock's film, and in Kieslowski's a sexually inexperienced adolescent focus a phallic telescope on his neighbour, we can now zoom in on a movie which adds a welcome element of comic eroticism to the filmic representations of this chapter's topic. As appropriate for a film about voyeurism, *Homework*[4] by Mexican filmmaker Jaime Humberto Hermosillo contains some nudity, erotic scenes, and frank conversations about sexuality which some viewers may feel uncomfortable about (which is probably all right) or even offended by (which is probably not). One of the film's two lead characters states somewhat defensively that "eroticism and good taste don't mix." I think they can, and they do here.

Homework is a low-budget feature with a deceptively simple structure, storyline and screenplay. When examined more closely, however, it emerges as a clever and entertaining work which presents, through a sophisticated use of the filmic language, a nonexploitative exploration of contemporary issues about couples and sexuality, as well as a witty self-reflection on the function of cinema itself. More specifically, it is quite exceptional in this genre because, while directed by a man, it considers voyeurism from the unusual perspective of a woman: the film school student Virginia (Maria Rojo), with whose point of view we are implicitly expected to identify.

In the two films previously discussed here I had focused on fragmentation (in *Rear Window*) and on a painful search for optimal distance (in *A Short Film about Love*) as their central metaphors. Here I would like instead to suggest that what is crucial to the formal structure and thematic content of *Homework* is the mechanism of *deception*. At first we are led to believe that it is Virginia who deceives her former lover Marcelo (José Alonso) by filming him *incognito*, having hidden a camcorder under a low table in preparation for his visit to her apartment. We the viewers are seduced to collude in her deception and become covert voyeurs ourselves. Seduction being, since Adam and Eve's days, the most powerful of traps, we are promised that we will be shown all the wonders of the Garden of Eden if only we allow ourselves to become her accomplices by letting our own point of view coincide with that of her camera. This last apparatus is cunningly placed to shoot, in real time and almost without any cuts, her anticipated romantic and passionate encounter with Marcelo. Witnesses of their reminiscences, we are then invited to share in their personal history, to let ourselves be embarrassed by eavesdropping on their trivialities and intimacies, to be moved by their affection for each other, to feel sympathy for their conflicts. The stuff life is made of.

When Marcelo nonchalantly places his jacket on the back of the chair and in front of the lens, thus depriving us of our voyeuristic pleasures until Virginia herself comes to put us out of our misery, we are painfully reminded of our impotent status. Indeed, passivity is an important component of our condition as spectators in general, and even more so of a film on voyeurism such as this, given the static perspective behind director Hermosillo's fixed camera. We are made to watch what we may not want to see, for instance scenes we may find disturbing, while at the same time we are not allowed to watch other scenes which we might have found exciting. We are back in the predicament of the child who is only partially protected from, or rather partially exposed to, the Primal Scene – the prototype scenario, that is, of all polymorphous perversity. Peeping through doors left ajar we can only see fragments of bodies; we see legs, shoulders, feet, fetishistic part objects rather than real whole persons.

About halfway into the film Marcelo becomes suspicious: "I have a feeling someone's watching us," he says (what an ironic statement! Of course, all of us film spectators are watching him). Upon discovering Virginia's camera with its red light on, he gets enraged at her deception and knocks the camera sideways, forcing us for a few minutes to view everything from a diagonal slant, again emphasizing our condition of paralysis. We must then painfully come to terms with the fact that Marcelo, having now come back to retrieve his briefcase, is quite pleased to be seduced into playing an active role in Virginia's secret project, narcissistically flexing his muscles and improvising a speech on women, life, sex, and so forth in front of her camcorder, as if it were just a mirror.

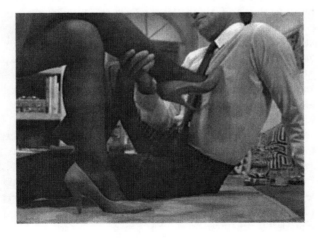

Figure 6.3 Homework (Hermosillo 1990)

Fixed behind its eyepiece, our point of view has remained the same; but we are no longer just on Virginia's side because we must accept that by now, not needing us any longer, she has moved away from us and into Marcelo's open arms. The pre-Oedipal infant immersed in the delusional fantasy of an omnipotently dyadic and symbiotic intercourse with mother has to grow up into the Oedipal child with an awareness of triangular constellations involving his or her exclusion from the parental relationship, other than as a curious, voyeuristic spectator of it. This developmental step, inevitable and rewarding as it is for psychological maturation, brings nevertheless with it a sense of betrayal, as children realize that their original fantasies could never be realized outside their minds insofar as a third party is also always going to be present.

Let us go back to our homework. Marcelo has, in the meantime, become fully conscious of the filming taking place, and once his virility has recovered from some initial humiliation he willingly incorporates the modicum of exhibitionism guaranteed by the presence of the video camera into their by now athletic sexual games. These take place on a hammock stretched across the room and are only partially visible from our fixed position and, briefly, through a veil draped like a filter over the lens. Again, we are left feeling that we are allowed to see both too much and not enough. When the sex gymnastics are over (the only overlong sequence, by the way, in an otherwise remarkably gripping slow-paced film) and Marcelo and Virginia get ready to part, everything makes us believe the film has reached its end.

But, again, we have been deceived, and this time by an unpredictable and uncannily Pirandellian twist of events. Virginia and Marcelo, as we are at long last allowed to discover, are but fictional characters created by two actors, Maria and Pepe Partida, playing their parts for a film project. We are left stunned by the realization that what we have seen so far is not at all what we were led to believe it was: the comedy we have hitherto been watching has turned, with a dramatic change of register, into Señor and Señora Partida's homemade video. We, the viewers, are forced to reconsider our own assumptions about what is actual and what is construction; what is feature, cinema vérité, or documentary; what is erotica and what pornography; what is an amateurish game and what a professional production. Chinese boxes-inside-boxes, Russian *babushkas*-inside-*babushkas,* Mexican films-inside-films. Or, in other words, these different levels of representation of reality lead us to challenge our relationship to it, and therefore our own values and identities.

The film eventually comes to an end. But as we reflect on our experience as spectators we realize that another, even deeper form of deception has taken place throughout, not to do with this particular film, but with *all* films. What we have been watching is not, or not only, Virginia's recording of her meeting with Marcelo as homework for her film school. What we have been watching is not, or not only, Maria and Pepe's joint pornographic video about Virginia and Marcelo's encounter, intended to lift their lives from boredom and improve their financial situation. Instead, what we have been watching for eighty-five minutes is also, or perhaps only, Jaime Humberto Hermosillo's carefully staged studio production, with leading actors José Alonso and Maria Rojo, intended for commercial distribution around the world.

And then we are left having to admit, yet again, that cinema, which we all love from here to eternity, is but an illusion: shadows and coloured shapes of light filtered through a steadily moving celluloid strip and projected onto a screen. For, and this must be our ultimate deception, nothing else is really there.

*****

When watching a movie, is our point of view always located behind the film-maker's camera? Does it necessarily coincide with that of the main character? How much of our self is left sitting in the cinema's chair and how much of it is transported, as it were, onto the screen? If there is an oscillation in this double register of identifications, when and why does it take place?

Mark (Karl Boehm), the protagonist of Michael Powell's *Peeping Tom*,[5] is a well-mannered psychopath. We watch him stabbing women to death with the tripod of his camera in order to film their expression of terror. We learn that as a child he had been subjected to cruel experiments by his father, a biologist researching human responses to fear. His young neighbour Helen (Anna Massey) and her wise, blind mother try unsuccessfully to understand his bizarre behaviour in order to rescue him. In the final scene Mark, by now pursued by the police, spectacularly kills himself in the same fashion in which he had murdered his victims.

In the terrific opening sequence of this movie Powell places us in a fascinatingly paradoxical situation: not only behind his own camera filming *Peeping Tom,* but also, collusively, behind the viewfinder of the protagonist's half-hidden Super-Eight, recording his own sadistic murders. Mark's camera is a phallic and deadly weapon, literally "shooting" its targeted preys with the help of its infernal paraphernalia: the sharpened tripod leg perforating his victims' throats and the mirror reflecting their terrorized gazes back to them. In the process his essentially covert voyeurism is turned into a collusive one; though here, of course, the objects are forced by his perversion into becoming exhibitionists against their own wishes. Mark's victims (a prostitute, a model and an actress: women whose activities already include a measure of narcissistic exhibitionism) are as vulnerable as he was himself as a child. The camera, and we suspect the projector as well, come then to represent the power of evil to seduce and destroy, and the cinema screen becomes a looking glass where we, the viewers, are made to witness our own wishes and fears reflected back at us in the characters with whom we identify.

As we are propelled by the film into a no-man's-land between the two cameras, a splitting process is imposed upon us whereby our visual and psychological place gets dislodged from what would otherwise be a more comfortable position. Such forced *dislocation* of perspective, and therefore of identification, and therefore of moral involvement, is what makes Powell's *Peeping Tom* so disturbing to us. This disturbance, I would suggest, is quite different from that induced by the fragmentation characterizing Hitchcock's *Rear Window* or the deceptions in Hermosillo's *Homework*.

In *Peeping Tom* this grey area of dislocation is even more complex than it at first appears. For if it concerns an ambiguous oscillation between the spaces behind the two cameras, it also relates to a similarly ambiguous oscillation between the spaces in front of the two projectors: the one before our eyes when we watch *Peeping Tom,* and the one in Mark's darkroom. A dark room indeed! Half-hidden behind a thick curtain, this is no Winnicottian transitional space of play and creativity but a place, symbolic as it is real, representing (in spite of being located upstairs and not, contrary to our topographical expectations, in an underground cellar) the Unconscious itself, full as it is of irrationality, repressed sexuality, deception and violence, and charged with intense Primal Scene and pre-Oedipal connotations. I will add that it is no coincidence that this room, as we learn, originally belonged to Mark's abusive father, while in contrast with it, the bedroom downstairs (once his mother's) represents a less primitive and more Oedipal space. It is here that Mark reluctantly lets Helen store his deadly camera before they go out together for dinner. He knows that she, by removing his weapon, is castrating him of his murderous pregenital sexuality and replacing it with a potential for romantic love – a condition desirable to her but terrifying to him because it challenges at its roots his own misogynous, predatory identity. We have learned by now that Mark is unredeemable by Helen's innocent affection or, later, by the therapeutic efforts of her farsighted, blind mother.[6] By daring to explore his lair (that is, by attempting to get closer to the darker corners of his mind), these Beauties only make themselves more vulnerable to become the Beast's next targets.

Peeping Tom presents us with an array of different forms of deviant sexuality and psychopathology: scopophilia, obsession with pornography, sadism and psychopathy, not to mention a deep depression underlying everything else. The cinematic gesture of linking them together in Mark's disordered personality seems to confirm Robert Stoller's view that perversion (indeed, all sexuality) is intrinsically characterized by a wish to humiliate and hurt: "I found that hostility – the urge to harm one's sexual object – was a central dynamic" (Stoller 1979, p. xii), he writes. Through the sexual act "frustration and trauma are converted to triumph, and, in fantasy, the victim of childhood is revenged" (Stoller 1979, p. 9).

Mark's voyeurism sadistically destroys his victims by literally penetrating them. It is clearly motivated by hatred, in contrast with the one we have come across in Kieslowski's *A Short Film about Love*. Mark's women, for all his charming manners, remain bodies to be hated. It is then understandable, much as it is regrettable, that *Peeping Tom* so unanimously enraged film critics when it opened in London in 1960 – the same year, incidentally, when another famous film on a psychopathic character was released, Hitchcock's *Psycho*. Powell's film, and Powell himself, were attacked not because its content, gory without spilling a single drop of blood, was too morbid for its time. Neither was *Peeping Tom*

Figure 6.4 Anna Massey in *Peeping Tom* (Powell 1960)

vilified because of the pessimistic considerations one could draw from it about the function of cinema as a whole (including the role possibly played by distressing film images in the perpetration of vicious crimes). No, the outrage arose because, being a film "where the process of film-making becomes an accessory to the crime" (Scorsese 1980), it stabbed the narcissistic movie establishment at its heart by depicting both film-lovers and filmmakers as voyeurs.

In its favor, there were places in *Peeping Tom* where a melodramatic *mise-en-scène* followed acceptable aesthetic conventions, or where the screenplay's dim subject was lit up with a healthy sense of self-referential flashes of humour. But these graces were not enough to save Powell's brilliant and prolific career (he was only to make three more films before his death in 1990). Nor was it helpful to Powell that he tried to give a psychological explanation to Mark's crimes by presenting them as cries of rage against his sadistic father, as well as rehearsals for his own approaching self-destruction.

The excitement of fear is the driving force at the source of both Mark's and his father's perversions; and to produce documentaries on the effects of fright on its victims is the project that links them together, or rather ties them in an inextricable knot. Powell's film thus indirectly raises questions about the long-lasting consequences of early parental influence.[7] But does such a psychogenetic explanation (which equates Mark to the monstrous creation of a Doctor Frankenstein) also provide an ethical justification to his deeds? Is he – and indirectly are we, as voyeuristic spectators – responsible? Why does Mark's suicide on his own sword, or camera, in a pyrotechnic frenzy of flash-bulbs, mirrors and audiotaped screams from his childhood, bring us spectators so much relief? It is, perhaps, because it allows us to avoid answering such unbearable questions.

Notes

1. *Rear Window* (United States 1954). Directed by Alfred Hitchcock. Written by John M. Hayes, from Cornell Woolrich's short story. Starring James Stewart (Jefferies), Grace Kelly (Lisa), and Raymond Burr (Lars Thorwald).
2. *A Short Film about Love [Krotki Film O Milosci]* (Poland 1988). Directed by Krzysztof Kieslowski. Written by Krzysztof Kieslowski and Krzysztof Piesiewicz. Starring Grazina Szapolowska (Magda), Olaf Lubaszenko (Tomek), and Stefania Iwinska (the landlady).
3. It might be of interest to note here that Kieslowski was diffident about psychoanalysis: "I'm very unfashionable about such things," he wrote, "I'm just as fanatically afraid of [psychoanalysts and psychotherapists] as I am of politicians, of priests, and of teachers" (in Stok 1993, p. 36) – practitioners, coincidentally, of professions which Freud (1937a) considered, alongside psychoanalysis, to be "impossible" ones.
4. *Homework [La tarea]* (Mexico 1990). Directed and written by Jaime Humberto Hermosillo. Starring Maria Rojo (Virginia) and José Alonso (Marcelo).
5. *Peeping Tom* (Great Britain 1960). Directed by Michael Powell. Written by Leo Marks. Starring Karl Boehm (Mark), Anna Massey (Helen), Moira Shearer (Vivian).
6. The blind seer is a *topos* derived from classical tragedy (e.g. Tyresias in Sophocles' *Oedipus Tyrannus*) and present in other films too (e.g. Nicolas Roeg's *Don't Look Now* 1973).
7. In the documentary which Mark shows to Helen, it is Michael Powell and his son Columba who ironically, or some would say perversely, play in *Peeping Tom* the parts of the biologist and of Mark as a child.

A last few words

This psychoanalytically informed exploration of cinema, framed within chapters on general themes of special interest to psychoanalysis, has given us an opportunity to revisit, or even discover, some of the many masterpieces this medium has produced in the course of its brief history.

My criterion for selecting which films, among the countless available, to present and discuss here has been as arbitrary as my choice of psychoanalytic ideas relevant to their interpretation. Unsystematic as this may inevitably appear to be, I would hope that the picture emerging from this journey beyond the couch may provide a justification to the interdisciplinary dialogue here entertained between the disparate cultural worlds of cinema and psychoanalysis – as well as an encouragement to further pursue it. Whenever such a constructive dialogue is established between them, it becomes apparent that each has something important to offer to, and gain from, the other. Analytic theories, rooted as they are in in-depth clinical work and in the detailed observation of, and reflection about, psychological phenomena, can lend their conceptual tools to original perspectives on film. Cinema in turn can respond to psychoanalysis by giving its practitioners new insights on a variety of human experiences.

French film scholar André Bazin famously asked the simple question, *"Qu'est-ce que le cinema?"* ("What is cinema?"). He knew that it was well worth asking, even if fundamentally unanswerable. Similarly, we could feel entitled to ask the parallel question, "What is psychoanalysis?" while anticipating only incomplete answers. (A colleague humorously dodged it by stating that "psychoanalysis is what psychoanalysts get trained to do!")

Cinema is more than the films we love to watch on a screen. It is also the ideas inspiring them, the reactions they evoke in their spectators, the creativity and craftsmanship and passionate commitment of large numbers of cast and crew bringing them to life. Psychoanalysis, on its part, is more than what takes place within the walls of a therapist's consulting room. It is also a sophisticated developmental psychology, a tool for researching the deeper corners of the human mind, and a set of theoretical concepts which can be helpfully applied to other fields and disciplines, cinema included. In W. H. Auden's words, psychoanalysis is "a whole climate of opinion."

I have already referred in my Introduction to the role played by curiosity in our interest in cinema and psychoanalysis, that odd couple. The curiosity which has now led us to ask those "What is" questions also seems well justified. It is indeed curiosity that motivates some people to make films, and others to watch them. It is curiosity that motivates some individuals to become psychoanalysts, and others to lie on their couches. And it is again because of their curiosity that some are drawn to write down their reflections on the complex and fascinating relationship between psychoanalysis and cinema, and others may be drawn to read them.

Appendix

FILM DIRECTORS

Pedro Almodóvar, the most talented and successful Spanish filmmaker along-side Luis Buñuel, was born in Calzada in 1949. At sixteen he moved to Madrid to study and make films, but ended up employed in an administrative job. While holding that job, he was making his first shorts, writing stories, playing in drag in a punk-rock band, acting on stage, and becoming a star of *la Movida*, the popular Madrid countercultural movement. In 1980 he made his first feature, *Pepi, Luci, Bom*, to be followed by, among others, *The Law of Desire* (1986), *Women on the Verge* (1988), *High Heels* (1991), *Live Flesh* (1997), *All About My Mother* (1999), *Talk to Her* (2002), *Bad Education* (2004), *Volver* (2006), *Broken Embraces* (2009) and *The Skin I Live In* (2011).

Hugh Brody was born in Sheffield and studied philosophy, politics, and economics at Oxford University. He was a lecturer in philosophy at Queens' University in Belfast before turning to anthropology and doing field research in remote Irish villages and with Northern Canadian Indians. This anthropological work resulted in a number of books (including *Maps and Dreams* and *The Other Side of Eden*) and documentaries. He holds the Canada Research Chair at the University of Frazer Valley and is an associate of the Scott Polar Research Institute at Cambridge University. *Nineteen Nineteen* is his first fictional feature film.

Luis Buñuel was born in Spain in 1900. His first films, *Un Chien Andalou* (1928) and *L'Age d'Or* (1930), were controversial works realized in collaboration with surrealist artist Salvador Dalí. Buñuel emigrated to Mexico and directed a variety of films, including melodramas, comedies, musicals and the ground-breaking *Los Olvidados* (1950). Some of his other masterpieces, such as *Viridiana* (1961) and *The Exterminating Angel* (1962) and the five films he directed in Europe after *Belle de Jour* – including *Tristana* (1970), *The Discreet Charm of the Bourgeoisie* (1972) and *That Obscure Object of Desire* (1977) – confirmed his popularity and his status as one of the most original filmmakers of the twentieth century. He died in Mexico City in 1983.

Claude Chabrol was born in Paris in 1930 in a middle-class family and died in 2010. He started as a film critic. In the late 1950s he began directing movies within the *Nouvelle Vague* experimental style, like several others of his colleagues writing for the *Cahiers du Cinéma*. Chabrol's best-known films from this period are *Le Beau Serge* (1958) and *Les Cousins* (1959) starring Stéphane Audran – his wife between 1964 and 1980. Out of Chabrol's vast production of over sixty films, we should mention *Les Bonnes Femmes* (1960), *Les Biches* (1968) and *The Unfaithful Wife* (1969) (also with Audran) and, with Isabelle Huppert, *Violette Nozière* (1978).

Guillermo del Toro was born in 1964 in Guadalajara. In the early years of his career he made short movies, produced and directed television programs, taught film studies, and wrote articles for film journals. His features include *Cronos* (1993), *Mimic* (1997), *The Devil's Backbone* (2001) and three Hollywood films inspired by comic books: *Blade II* (2002), *Hellboy* (2004) and *Hellboy II* (2008).

Victor Erice was born in 1940 in a village in the Spanish region of Biscay. He studied law, political science and economics at the University of Madrid, and film direction at the Escuela Oficial de Cinematografia. He wrote film criticism and directed some shorts before his first feature, *The Spirit of the Beehive*. After a nine-year gap Erice wrote and directed his second film, *The South* (1982) and after another long gap *The Quince Tree Sun* (1992), a documentary about painter Antonio López Garçia.

Born in 1920 in Rimini, **Federico Fellini** moved in 1939 to Rome, the location of some of his most memorable films, including *Cabiria* (1956), *La Dolce Vita* (1960) and *Roma* (1972). Autobiographical events from his childhood in Rimini (represented in *I vitelloni* 1953 and *Amarcord* 1973) as well as imagined stories and dreams became material for much of his work. *La strada* (1954) and *Cabiria* (1956) were influenced by *Neorealismo*. Jung's theories on archetypes and the collective unconscious provided material for *8 1/2* (1963), *Juliet of the Spirits* (1965), *Satyricon* (1969), *Casanova* (1970) and *City of Women* (1980). Months before he died in 1993 Fellini was given the Academy Honorary award for his unique contribution to world cinema.

Frédéric Fonteyne is a Belgian filmmaker born in 1968. As well as several shorts, his films include *Max et Bobo* (1997), *La Femme de Gilles* (2004) and *Tango Libre* (2012).

Jaime Humberto Hermosillo is a successful Mexican director whose main focus is to expose the hypocrisies of the middle classes. Among his films are *Dona Herlinda and Her Son* (1985), *La Tarea Prohibida* (1992), *De Noche Vienes, Esmeralda* (1997) and *Juventud* (2010).

Alfred Hitchcock was born in the East End of London in 1899 and received a strict Catholic education. His first movie was *The Pleasure Garden* (1925), followed by *The Lodger* (1927) and other films such as *The Lady Vanishes* (1938). American producer David O. Selznick invited him to the United States, where Hitchcock's first film was *Rebecca* (1940), followed by a long string of international successes such as *Notorious* (1946), *Strangers on a Train* (1951), *Rear Window* (1954), *Vertigo* (1958), *North by Northwest* (1959), *Psycho* (1960), *The*

Birds (1963), *Marnie* (1964) and *Frenzy* (1972). French critics of the *Nouvelle Vague,* notably Chabrol and Truffaut, contributed to his reputation as a formidable auteur, and not just as a "Master of Suspense." Hitchcock died in Beverly Hills in 1980.

Alejandro Gonzales Iñarritu was born in Mexico City in 1963. In the 1980s he composed soundtracks for six Mexican feature films; in the 1990s he worked on a large number of commercials. He collaborated with screenwriter Guillermo Arriaga on *Amores Perros* (2000), *21 Grams* (2003) and *Babel* (2006), and wrote his next film, *Biutiful* (2010). His movies have won prestigious international awards and have starred such major actors as Gael García Bernal, Benicio del Toro, Naomi Watts, Sean Penn, Brad Pitt, Cate Blanchett and Xavier Bardem.

Peter Jackson was born in New Zealand in 1961. His films include: *Bad Taste* (1987), *Meet the Feebles* (1989), *Braindead* (1992), *The Frighteners* (1996), *King Kong* (2005) and the trilogy of blockbusters *Lord of the Rings: The Fellowship of the Ring* (2001), *Lord of the Rings: The Two Towers* (2002) and *Lord of the Rings: The Return of the King* (2003).

Krzysztof Kieslowski was born in Warsaw in 1941 and died in 1996. Like the other major Polish directors – Wajda, Polanski, Skolimowsy and Zanussi – he trained at the Lodz Film School, from which he graduated in 1969. After making a number of documentaries and feature films, Kieslowski acquired international success in 1988 with *The Decalogue*. After moving to France, he directed *The Double Life of Veronique* (1991) and the trilogy *Three Colours: Blue, White, Red* (1993–1994).

Ken Loach was born in England in 1936. He studied law at Oxford and worked in the theatre. With producer Tony Garnett he directed several Wednesday Plays for television, such as the influential *Cathy Come Home* (1966). His many films, almost fifty so far, include *Poor Cow* (1967), *Hidden Agenda* (1990), *Ladybird Ladybird* (1994), *Land and Freedom* (1995), *The Wind that Shakes the Barley* (2006) and *Looking for Eric* (2009).

Brazilian screenwriter, producer and film director **Fernando Meirelles** was born in São Paulo in 1955 and trained as an architect. He worked in advertising before making films. These include *The Constant Gardener* (2005) and *Blindness* (2008) from José Saramago's novel.

Lukas Moodysson was born in Sweden in 1969. Also the author of several books of verse and narrative, his films include *Show Me Love* (1998), *Together* (2000) and *Mammoth* (2008), as well as experimental and controversial works such as *A Hole in My Hearth* (2004) and *Container* (2006). He is a committed Christian, but also an outspoken supporter of left-wing politics and feminism.

Georg Wilhelm Pabst, one of the great European filmmakers of the 1920s and 1930s and a major exponent of German Expressionism in cinema, was born in Austria in 1885 and died in Vienna in 1967. His films include *The Joyless Street* (1925), *Pandora's Box* (1928) and *The Threepenny Opera* (1931).

Michael Powell was born in Kent in 1905. Most of his movies were written and directed in collaboration with Emeric Pressburger in the 1940s and 1950s, under the banner of *The Archers*. These films include *A Matter of Life and Death* (1946), *Black Narcissus* (1947) and *The Red Shoes* (1948). He died in 1990.

Michael Radford was born in New Delhi in 1946 and educated at Oxford University. His films include *Another Time, Another Place* (1983), *1984* (1984), *Dancing at the Blue Iguana* (2000), *The Merchant of Venice* (2004) and documentaries about *Van Morrison in Ireland* (1980) and jazz pianist *Michel Petrucciani* (2011).

Roberto Rossellini was born in Rome in 1906. He is considered a major influence on world cinema, but most of his large body of work, much of it produced for television, is unknown to the general public. The exceptions are *Roma, Open City* (1945), *Paisà* (1946) and two of the films starring his wife Ingrid Bergman: *Stromboli* (1949) and *Viaggio in Italia* (1953). Rossellini's filmography also includes: *La nave bianca* (1941), *Un pilota ritorna* (1942), *Dov'è la libertà?* (1954), *Giovanna d'Arco al rogo* (1954), *Il generale Della Rovere* (1959), *Vanina Vanini* (1961), *La lotta dell'uomo per la sua sopravvivenza* (1964–1970), *La prise de pouvoir par Louis XIV* (1966) and *Il Messia* (1975). He died in 1977.

Carlos Saura was born in Spain in 1932. He has directed a large number of successful films, including *La Caza* (1966), *Cousin Angelica* (1974), *Mama Turns 100* (1979), *Carmen* (1983), *The Dark Night of the Soul* (1989), *¡Ay, Carmela!* (1990), *Shoot!* (1993), *Flamenco* (1995), *Tango* (1998) and *Goya in Bordeaux* (1999).

John Schlesinger was born in London in 1926 into a middle-class family. He studied at Oxford University and worked for years as an actor before becoming a film director. His movies include *Billy Liar* (1963), *Darling* (1965), *Far From the Madding Crowd* (1967), *Sunday, Bloody Sunday* (1971), *The Day of the Locust* (1974), *Marathon Man* (1976) and *The Next Best Thing* (2000). He also directed plays, musicals, and operas. He died in 2003.

Zornitsa Sophia was born in 1972 in Bulgaria and graduated from the National Academy of Fine Arts in Sofia in 1996. In 1997 she specialized in fine arts at the School of Visual Arts, New York, and in advertising and graphic design at the American University, Washington, D.C. In 2002 she specialized in film and TV directing at NAFTA in Sofia, under the supervision of Lyudmil Staykov. *Mila from Mars* (2004) was followed by *Death and All the Way Back* (2005), *Modus Vivendi* (2007), *Forecast* (2008) and *Love Building* (2013).

Luchino Visconti was born in Milan in 1906 and died in 1976. A stark realist in his early films, he became increasingly attracted to the opulent decadence of romantic melodrama and to the best literature of the turn of the century. This is evident in the choice of authors who inspired his films: from the *verista* Giovanni Verga for *La Terra Trema* (1948) to the dandy Gabriele D'Annunzio for *The Innocent* (his last film, 1976), via Dostojevski (*Le notti bianche*), Camus (*The Outsider*) and Thomas Mann (*Death in Venice*).

FILMOGRAPHY

L'Age d'Or (Buñuel 1930)
American Beauty (Mendes 1999)
Amores Perros (Iñarritu 2000)
Bad Taste (Jackson 1987)
Barton Fink (Coen Brothers 1991)
Belle de Jour (Buñuel 1967)
Bellissima (Visconti 1951)
Black Orpheus (Camus 1959)
Le Boucher (Chabrol 1970)
Braindead (Jackson 1992)
Breakfast at Tiffany's (Edwards 1961)
The Cabinet of Dr Caligari (Wiene 1920)
Cabiria (Fellini 1956)
To Catch a Thief (Hitchcock 1955)
Central Station (Salles 1998)
La Cérémonie (Chabrol 1995)
Un Chien Andalou (Buñuel 1928)
Cinema Paradiso (Tornatore 1988)
City of God (Meirelles 2002)
Un Coeur en Hiver (Sautet 1991)
The Conformist (Bertolucci 1970)
Cose da pazzi (Pabst 1953)
Cría Cuervos (Saura 1976)
Cronos (del Toro 1993)
A Dangerous Method (Cronenberg 2011)
Day for Night (Truffaut 1973)
Deconstructing Harry (Allen 1997)
The Deer Hunter (Cimino 1978)
The Devil's Backbone (del Toro 2001)
The Diary of a Chambermaid (Buñuel 1964)
Dirty Pretty Things (Frears 2002)
Distant (Ceylan 2002)
La Dolce Vita (Fellini 1960)
Don't Look Now (Roeg 1973)
Double Indemnity (Wilder 1944)
Duel in the Sun (Vidor 1946)
El (Buñuel 1952)
The Exterminating Angel (Buñuel 1962)
Family Life (Loach 1969)
Festen (Vinterberg 1998)
The 400 Blows (Truffaut 1959)
Frankenstein (Whale 1931)

Frenzy (Hitchcock 1972)
Freud: The Secret Passion (Huston 1962)
Germany Year Zero (Rossellini 1948)
Goodfellas (Scorsese 1990)
The Hairdresser's Husband (Leconte 1990)
Happiness (Solondz 1998)
Heavenly Creatures (Jackson 1994)
Homework (Hermosillo 1990)
Inconscientes (Oristrell 2004)
In Treatment (various directors 2010)
Jagged Edge (Marquand 1985)
Jeanne Dielman (Akermann 1975)
The Joyless Street (Pabst 1925)
Kes (Loach 1969)
The Kid with a Bike (Dardenne Brothers 2011)
Klute (Pakula 1971)
Kolya (Sveràk 1996)
Last Tango in Paris (Bertolucci 1972)
Leaving Las Vegas (Figgis 1995)
La Lectrice (Delville 1988)
Lilya-4-Ever (Moodysson 2002)
Little Otik (Svankmajer 2000)
The Lodger (Hitchcock 1927)
Marnie (Hitchcock 1964)
Matador (Almodóvar 1986)
My Name Was Sabina Spielrein (Màrton 2002)
Midnight Cowboy (Schlesinger 1969)
Mila from Mars (Sophia 2004)
Mona Lisa (Jordan 1986)
My Own Executioner (Kimmins 1948)
The Mystery of the Rocks of Kador (Perret 1912)
Nineteen Nineteen (Brody 1985)
North by Northwest (Hitchcock 1959)
Notorious (Hitchcock 1946)
The Odd Couple (Saks 1968)
Of Mice and Men (Milestone 1939)
Los Olvidados (Buñuel 1950)
One Flew over the Cuckoo's Nest (Forman 1975)
Orphée (Cocteau 1950)
Paisà (Rossellini 1946)
Pandora's Box (Pabst 1928)
Pan's Labyrinth (del Toro 2006)
Peeping Tom (Powell 1960)

Ponette (Doillon 1996)
A Pornographic Affair (Fonteyne 1999)
Il Postino (Radford 1994)
Pretty Woman (Marshall 1990)
Psycho (Hitchcock 1960)
Pulp Fiction (Tarantino 1994)
Rear Window (Hitchcock 1954)
Rebecca (Hitchcock 1940)
Record of a Tenement's Gentleman (Ozu 1947)
Le Retour de Martin Guerre (Vigne 1982)
Rome, Open City (Rossellini 1945)
Saboteur (Hitchcock 1942)
Sauve qui Peut (Godard 1980)
Schindler's List (Spielberg 1993)
Secrets of a Soul (Pabst 1926)
Seven (Fincher 1995)
Shock Corridor (Fuller 1963)
A Short Film about Killing (Kieslowski 1988)
A Short Film about Love (Kieslowski 1988)
Sigmund Freud: His Family and Colleagues, 1928–1947 (Lehman 1985)
The Skin I Live In (Almodóvar 2011)
The Snake Pit (Litvak 1948)
The Son's Room (Moretti 2001)
The Sopranos (Chase 1999–2007)
The Soul Keeper (Faenza 2003)
Spellbound (Hitchcock 1945)
Spirit of the Beehive (Erice 1973)
Strangers on a Train (Hitchcock 1951)
Surviving Life (Svankmajer 2010)
Suspicion (Hitchcock 1941)
Talk to Her (Almodóvar 2002)
The Third Man (Reed 1949)
The 39 Steps (Hitchcock 1935)
The Three Faces of Eve (Johnson 1957)
Titanic (Cameron 1997)
Tristana (Buñuel 1970)
Vertigo (Hitchcock 1958)
With a Friend Like Harry . . . (Moll 2000)
The Wizard of Oz (Fleming 1938)
The Wrong Man (Hitchcock 1956)

GLOSSARY OF PSYCHOANALYTIC TERMS

- **Archetypes** For Carl G. Jung, the innate symbolic prototypes of ideas or characters (such as the Great Mother or the Wise Old Man) shared universally in the collective unconscious.
- **Castration Anxiety** A child's common fear of punishment, in retaliation for sexual and aggressive fantasies during the Oedipus complex stage of development.
- **Condensation** The unconscious process of creating a single object, word or person having two or more meanings (*In a dream, Bob's wife has the same looks or name as his mother*).
- **Core Complex** For Mervin Glasser, the anxiety of abandonment and engulfment experienced by the child at separation from the mother, also a feature in sexual deviations.
- **Countertransference** The analyst's unconscious response to the patient's transference.
- **Deferred Action** (Nachträglichkeit in German, Après coup in French) The distorted recollection in the present of memories from the past.
- **Denial** The belief that something unpleasant does not exist or has never happened.
- **Displacement** When feelings or ideas are transferred from the original object to a more acceptable substitute (*When Lucy is angry with her husband, she shouts instead at her daughter*).
- **Identification** The delusional belief or wish to be someone else, often an idealized person.
- **Lack** (*Manque* in the original French) For Jacques Lacan, it is the necessary condition for the experience of desire.
- **Objects and Object Relations** People as we experience them, and how they interact with us and each other, in our mental space.
- **Oedipus Complex** The universal attraction of a child for one parent and jealousy of the other, later extended to other triangular relationships.
- **Paranoid-Schizoid Position** For Melanie Klein, the earliest state of the baby, when he splits the breast into two: a good one and a bad one. In contrast, a child in the more advanced **Depressive Position** has ambivalent feelings towards the same good-and-bad mother.
- **Parapraxis** Any form of meaningful everyday-life psychopathology such as slips of the tongue, forgetting names and losing objects.
- **Pleasure Principle and Reality Principle** The infantile wish for immediate gratification (Pleasure Principle) is later partially replaced by the Reality Principle allowing the child to wait for a more satisfactory outcome (*A chicken tomorrow may be better than an egg today*).
- **Primal Scene** The observed or imagined intercourse between the parents, often experienced by the child as both exciting and frightening.

- **Primary Process** The set of principles (such as timelessness or absence of contradictions) dominating the functioning of the Unconscious, as opposed to **Secondary Process** logic dominating the functioning of the conscious mind.
- **Projection** The attribution of one's unacceptable feelings, ideas and so forth to someone else (*Instead of feeling envious of his friend Jim for his success with girlfriends, Bob experienced Jim as being envious of him for his money*).
- **Projective identification** The double process of attributing one's own feelings to another person, and then identifying with him/her.
- **Regression** Going back in time to earlier experiences or ways of functioning (*A four-year old child becomes incontinent again after the birth of his little brother*).
- **Repression** The process of removing from conscious awareness unpleasant realities or experiences. Repressed material can reemerge to consciousness in a disguised form (e.g. as a dream, a symptom, a parapraxis).
- **Royal Road** (to the Unconscious). That's how Freud describes the process of dream interpretation.
- **Secondary Revision** The artificial reordering of the contents of a dream in order to better disguise the unconscious wishes it had tried to express.
- **Seduction Theory** Freud's original (but later refuted) belief that adult neurotic symptoms always stem from instances of sexual abuse experienced during childhood.
- **Splitting** An early defense mechanism, resulting in starkly contrasting "good" with "bad" objects.
- **Sublimation** The unconscious process of using sexual and aggressive drives for socially acceptable (e.g. artistic and scientific) activities.
- **Superego** The component of the Structural Model (alongside Ego and Id) consisting of internalized laws, moral rules, taboos and other limitations to instinctual behaviour.
- **Symbolic Order** For Jacques Lacan, the world of linguistic communication, intersubjective relations and acceptance of the law (the Name of the Father). It works alongside the Imaginary Order and the Real.
- **Transference** The patient's unconscious attribution to the analyst of features, feelings, scenarios and so forth belonging to earlier internal objects (e.g. the parents).
- **Transitional Space** For Donald Winnicott, the imaginary space of play, creativity and analytic work, situated between the self and the external world.
- **Uncanny** (*Unheimlich* in German) A vast category of phenomena, disturbing while appearing to be familiar, related to primitive and repressed fears.
- **Unconscious** In the Topographical Model, the part of the mind unavailable to awareness (unlike the Conscious and the Preconscious) and the seat of repressed fantasies and defense mechanisms.

References

Abraham, K. (1922) The rescue and murder of the father in neurotic phantasies. *International Journal of Psycho-Analysis*, 3: 467–474.

Abraham, H. and Freud, E. (Eds.) (1965) *A Psycho-Analytical Dialogue. The Letters of Sigmund Freud and Karl Abraham. 1907–1926*. London: Hogarth Press.

Almansi, R. (1992) Alfred Hitchcock's disappearing women: A study in scopophilia and object loss. *International Journal of Psycho-Analysis*, 19: 81–90.

Andrew, G. (2003) *BFI* interview with Victor Erice in "The quiet genius of Victor Erice". *Vertigo* 2(6), 2004.

Atwood, G.E. (1978) On the origins and dynamics of messianic salvation fantasies. *International Review of Psycho-Analysis*, 5: 85–96.

Barrie, J.M. (1911) *Peter Pan*. Ware: Wordsworth, 1993.

Benton, R. (1984) Film as dream: Alfred Hitchcock's *Rear Window. Psychoanalytic Review*, 71: 483–500.

Berardinelli, J. (1994) Review of *A Short Film about Love*. http://www.reelviews.net
—— (2000) Review of *An Affair of Love*. http://www.reelviews.net
—— (2007) Movie review of *Pan's Labyrinth*. http://www.reelviews.net

Bergan, R. (2010) Claude Chabrol's obituary. *The Guardian,* 12 September 2010.

Berger, J. (1985) Afterword. In Hugh Brody and Michael Ignatieff, *Nineteen Nineteen*. London: Faber & Faber.

Berman, E. (1997) Hitchcock's *Vertigo:* The collapse of a rescue fantasy. In *International Journal of Psycho-Analysis*, 78: 975–996.

Bergstrom, J. (Ed.) (1999) *Endless Night: Cinema and Psychoanalysis, Parallel Histories*. Los Angeles: University of California Press.

Bonaparte, M. (1954) The fault of Orpheus in reverse. *International Journal of Psycho-Analysis*, 35: 109–112.

Bradshaw, P. (2003) Review of *City of God*. In *The Guardian*, 3 January 2003.

Brandell, J.R. (2004) Eighty years of dream sequences: A cinematic journey down Freud's "Royal Road." *American Imago*, 61: 59–76.

Breuer, J., and Freud, S. (1893–1895) *Studies on Hysteria*. Translated from the German and edited by James Strachey. *The Standard Edition of the Complete Psychological Works of Sigmund Freud*, Vol. 2. London: Hogarth Press, 1955.

Breton, A. (1924) *Manifeste du Surréalisme*. Paris: Le Sagittaire.

Britton, A. (1985) *Spellbound:* Text and subtext. *CineAction!*, 3/4.

Brody, H., and Brearley, M. (2003) Filming psychoanalysis: Feature or documentary? Two contributions. In A. Sabbadini (Ed.) *The Couch and the Silver Screen. Psychoanalytic Reflections on European Cinema*. Hove: Brunner-Routledge.

Browne, N., and McPherson, B. (1980) Dream and photography in a psychoanalytic film: "Secrets of a Soul." *Dreamworks*, 1: 35–45.

Brunette, P. (1987) *Roberto Rossellini*. Oxford: Oxford University Press.

Buñuel, L. (1982) *My Last Breath*. London: Vintage, 1994.

Burnett, F. H. (1911) *The Secret Garden*. Ware: Wordsworth, 1993.

Cain, J. M. (1934) *The Postman Always Rings Twice*. London: Orion Books, 2010.

Carroll, L. (1865) *Alice's Adventures in Wonderland*. London: Macmillan, 1949.

Chasseguet-Smirgel, J. (1983) Perversion and the universal law. *International Review of Psycho-Analysis*, 10: 293–302.

Chodorkoff, B., and Baxter, S. (1974) "Secrets of a Soul": An early psychoanalytic film venture. *American Imago*, 31: 319–334.

Collodi, C. (1883) *Pinocchio*. London: Wordsworth, 1995.

Cooper, A. (1991) The unconscious core of perversion. In G. Fogel and W. Myers (Eds.) *Perversions and Near-Perversions in Clinical Practice*. New Haven: Yale University Press, 1991, pp. 17–35.

Cowie, E. (1997) *Representing the Woman: Cinema and Psychoanalysis*. London: Macmillan.

de Mijolla, A. (1994) Freud and the psychoanalytic situation on the screen. In J. Bergstrom (Ed.) *Endless Night: Cinema and Psychoanalysis, Parallel Histories*. Los Angeles: University of California Press, 1999.

Ebert, R. (2000) Review of *An Affair of Love*. http://rogerebert.suntimes.com

—— (2007) Review of *Pan's Labyrinth*. *Chicago Sun-Times*, 25 August 2007.

Eberwein, R. T. (1984) *Film and The Dream Screen: A Sleep and a Forgetting*. Princeton, NJ: Princeton University Press.

Edelson, M. (1993) Telling and enacting stories in psychoanalysis and psychotherapy. Implications for teaching psychotherapy. *Psychoanalytic Study of the Child*, 48: 293–325.

Ehrenburg, I. (1931) *Die Traumfabriki Chronik des Films*. Berlin: Malik.

Erikson, E. (1959) *Identity and the Life Cycle. Selected Papers*. New York: Norton, 1980.

Esman, A. H. (1987) Rescue fantasies. *Psychoanalytic Quarterly*, 56: 263–270.

Faldini, F. and Fofi, G. (1979) *L'avventurosa storia del cinema italiano raccontata dai suoi protagonisti (1935–1959)*. Milan: Feltrinelli.

Falzeder, E., and Brabant, E. (Eds.) (2000) *The Correspondence of Sigmund Freud and Sándor Ferenczi*. Vol. 3, *1920–1933*. Cambridge, MA: Belknap Press of Harvard Univ. Press.

Feinstein, H. (1996) Killer instincts: Director Claude Chabrol finds madness in his method. *The Village Voice*, 24 December 1996.

Fogel, G. (1991) Perversity and perverse: Updating a psychoanalytic paradigm. In G. Fogel and W. Myers (Eds.), *Perversions and Near-Perversions in Clinical Practice*. New Haven: Yale University Press, pp. 1–13.

Fogel, G. and Myers, W. (Eds.) (1991) *Perversions and Near-Perversions in Clinical Practice*. New Haven: Yale University Press.

French, P. (1985) Angst for the memory. *The Observer*, 15 December 1985, p. 17.

Freud, E. L. (Ed.) (1961) *Letters of Sigmund Freud 1873–1939*. London: Hogarth Press.

Freud, S. (1900) *The Interpretation of Dreams (First Part)*. Vol. 4 of *The Standard Edition of the Complete Psychological Works of Sigmund Freud*. Translated from the German and edited by James Strachey. London: Hogarth Press, 1953. (Hereafter *Standard Edition*.)

—— (1900–1901) *The Interpretation of Dreams (Second Part) and On Dreams*. Vol. 5 of *Standard Edition*. London: Hogarth Press, 1953.

—— (1901–1905) Three essays on the theory of sexuality. In *A Case of Hysteria, Three Essays on Sexuality and Other Works*. Vol. 7 of *Standard Edition*. London: Hogarth Press, 1953, pp. 123–246.

—— (1909) Analysis of a phobia in a five-year-old boy. In *Two Case Histories ("Little Hans" and the "Rat Man")*. Vol. 10 of *Standard Edition*. London: Hogarth Press, 1955, pp. 1–150.

—— (1910a) Leonardo da Vinci. A memory of his childhood. In *Five Lectures on Psycho-Analysis, Leonardo da Vinci and Other Works*. Vol. 11 of *Standard Edition*. London: Hogarth Press, 1957, pp. 57–138.

—— (1910b) A special type of choice of object made by men. In *Five Lectures on Psycho-Analysis, Leonardo da Vinci and Other Works*. Vol. 11 of *Standard Edition*. London: Hogarth Press, 1957, pp. 163–176.

—— (1913a) The theme of the Three Caskets. In *The Case of Schreber, Papers on Technique and Other Works*. Vol. 12 of *Standard Edition*. London: Hogarth Press, 1958, pp. 289–302.

—— (1913b) *Totem and Taboo and Other Works*. Vol. 13 of *Standard Edition*. London: Hogarth Press, 1955, pp. vii–162.

—— (1913c) On beginning the treatment. In *The Case of Schreber, Papers on Technique and Other Works*. Vol. 12 of *Standard Edition*. London: Hogarth Press, 1958, pp. 121–144.

—— (1914) The Moses of Michelangelo. In *Totem and Taboo and Other Works*. Vol. 13 of *Standard Edition*. London: Hogarth Press, 1955, pp. 209–238.

—— (1915) Instincts and their vicissitudes. In *On the History of the Psycho-Analytic Movement, Papers on Metapsychology and Other Works*. Vol. 14 of *Standard Edition*. London: Hogarth Press, 1957, pp. 109–140.

—— (1918) From the history of an infantile neurosis. In *An Infantile Neurosis and Other Works*. Vol. 17 of *Standard Edition*. London: Hogarth Press, 1955, pp. 1–124.

—— (1920a) Beyond the pleasure principle. In *Beyond the Pleasure Principle, Group Psychology and Other Works*. Vol. 18 of *Standard Edition*. London: Hogarth Press, 1955, pp. 1–64.

—— (1920b) The psychogenesis of a case of homosexuality in a woman. In *Beyond the Pleasure Principle, Group Psychology and Other Works*. Vol. 18 of *Standard Edition*. London: Hogarth Press, 1955, pp. 145–172.

—— (1923) Two encyclopaedia articles. In *Beyond the Pleasure Principle, Group Psychology and Other Works*. Vol. 18 of *Standard Edition*. London: Hogarth Press, 1955, pp. 233–260.

—— (1925a) A note upon the "Mystic Writing Pad." In *The Ego and the Id and Other Works*. Vol. 19 of *Standard Edition*. London: Hogarth Press, 1961, pp. 225–232.

—— (1925b) An autobiographical study. In *An Autobiographical Study, Inhibitions, Symptoms and Anxiety, The Question of Lay Analysis and Other Works*. Vol. 20 of *Standard Edition*. London: Hogarth Press, 1959, pp. 1–74.

—— (1927) Fetishism. In *The Future of an Illusion, Civilization and its Discontents, and Other Works*. Vol. 21 of *Standard Edition*. London: Hogarth Press, 1961, pp. 147–158.

—— (1930) Civilization and its discontents. In *The Future of an Illusion, Civilization and its Discontents, and Other Works*. Vol. 21 of *Standard Edition*. London: Hogarth Press, 1961, pp. 57–146.

———— (1937a) Analysis terminable and interminable. In *Moses and Monotheism, An Outline of Psycho-Analysis and Other Works*. Vol. 23 of *Standard Edition*. London: Hogarth Press, 1964, pp. 209–254.

———— (1937b) Constructions in analysis. In *Moses and Monotheism, An Outline of Psycho-Analysis and Other Works*. Vol. 23 of *Standard Edition*. London: Hogarth Press, 1964, pp. 255–270.

Friedberg, A. (1990) An *Unheimlich* maneuver between psychoanalysis and the cinema: "Secrets of a Soul" (1926). In E. Rentschler (Ed.) *The Films of G. W. Pabst. An Extraterritorial Cinema*. New Brunswick: Rutgers University Press.

Fromm, E. (1957) *The Art of Loving*. London: Unwin Books.

Frosch, J. (1959) Transference derivatives of the family romance. *Journal of the American Psychoanalytic Association*, 7: 503–522.

Fuller, G. (Ed.) (1998) *Loach on Loach*. London: Faber & Faber.

Gabbard, G. O. (1997) Guest editorial: The psychoanalyst at the movies. In *International Journal of Psycho-Analysis*, 78: 429–434.

Gabbard, G. O., and Gabbard, K. (1989) The female psychoanalyst in the movies. *Journal of the American Psychoanalytic Association*, 37: 1031–1049.

———— (1999) *Psychiatry and the Cinema*. 2nd ed. Washington, DC: American Psychiatric Press, 1999.

Gifford, S. (2004) Freud at the movies, 1907–1925: From the Piazza Colonna and Hammerstein's Roofgarden to *The Secrets of a Soul*. In J. Brandell (Ed.), *Celluloid Couches, Cinematic Clients: Psychoanalysis and Psychotherapy in the Movies*. Albany: State University of New York Press, 2004, pp. 147–168.

Gillman, R. D. (1992) Rescue fantasies and the secret benefactor. *Psychoanalytic Study of the Child*, 47: 279–298.

Glasser, M. (1986) Identification and its vicissitudes as observed in the perversions. *International Journal of Psycho-Analysis*, 67: 9–16.

Glenn, J. (1986) Twinship themes and fantasies in the work of Thornton Wilder. *Psychoanalytic Study of the Child*, 41: 627–651.

Goffman, I. (1961) *Asylums. Essays on the Social Situation of Mental Patients and Other Inmates*. New York: Anchor Books.

Graham, B. (1998) Fellini keeps giving and giving with "Cabiria." *San Francisco Chronicle*, 31 July 1998.

Greenacre, P. (1966) Problems of overidealization of the analyst and of analysis. *Psychoanalytic Study of the Child*, 21: 193–212.

Grinstein, A. (1957) A specific defense in psychoanalytic therapy: "Comes the knight in shining armor." *Journal of the American Psychoanalytic Association*, 5: 124–129.

Hines, B. (1968) *A Kestrel for a Knave*. London: Penguin, 2000.

Hinson, H. (1988) Matador (NR). *Washington Post*, 30 April 1988.

Hoffman, J. (1986) Can we talk? *Village Voice*, 30 September 1986, p. 70.

Johnson, T. (1993) *Hysteria, or Fragments of an Analysis of an Obsessional Neurosis*. London: Methuen Drama.

Jones, E. (1955) *Sigmund Freud. Life and Work*. Vol. 2, *Years of Maturity 1901–1919*. London: Hogarth Press.

———— (1957) *Sigmund Freud. Life and Work*. Vol. 3, *The Last Phase 1919–1939*. London: Hogarth Press.

Kaplan, L. (1991) Women masquerading as women. In G. Fogel and W. Myers (Eds.), *Perversions and Near-Perversions in Clinical Practice*. New Haven: Yale University Press, pp. 127–152.

Kermode, M. (2006) *Guardian/BFI* interview with Guillermo del Toro. http://www.theguardian.com/film/2006/nov/21/guardianinterviewsatbfisouthbank

Kernberg, O. (1991) Aggression and love in the relationship of the couple. In G. Fogel and W. Myers (Eds.), *Perversions and Near-Perversions in Clinical Practice*. New Haven: Yale University Press, pp. 153–175.

———— (1995) *Love Relations. Normality and Pathology*. New Haven: Yale University Press.

Khan, M. (1979) *Alienation in Perversion*. London: Maresfield Library, 1989.

Kline, T. J. (1976) Orpheus transcending: Bertolucci's *Last Tango in Paris. International Review of Psycho-Analysis*, 3: 85–95.

Laufer, M., and Laufer, E. (1984) *Adolescence and Developmental Breakdown. A Psychoanalytic View*. New Haven: Yale University Press.

Lewin, B. D. (1953) Reconsideration of the dream screen. *Psychoanalytic Quarterly*, 22: 174–199.

Limentani, A. (1989) The Orpheus myth as reflected in problems of ambivalence and reparation in the Oedipal situation. In *Between Freud and Klein. The Psychoanalytic Quest for Knowledge and Truth*. London: Karnac Books, 1998.

Loewald, H. (1960) On the therapeutic action of psychoanalysis. In *Papers on Psychoanalysis*. New Haven: Yale University Press, 1980, pp. 221–256.

MacDonald, S. (1990) Secrets of a soul: A psychoanalytic film. In P. Collier and J. Davies (Eds.) *Modernism and the European Unconscious*. Cambridge: Polity Press.

Maraini, D. (1973) *Only Prostitutes Marry in May*. Toronto: Guernica Editions, 1998.

Marcus, L. (2001) Dreaming and cinematographic consciousness. *Psychoanalysis and History*, 3: 51–68.

Marinelli, L. (2004) Smoking, laughing, and the compulsion to film: On the beginnings of psychoanalytic documentaries. *American Imago*, 61:35–58.

McCourt, F. (1996) *Angela's Ashes. A Memoir of a Childhood*. London: Flamingo.

McDougall, J. (1991) Perversions and deviations in the psychoanalytic attitude. In G. Fogel and W. Myers (Eds.), *Perversions and Near-Perversions in Clinical Practice*. New Haven: Yale University Press, pp. 176–203.

Merigliano, D. (2010) "Il labirinto del fauno" e "La spina del diavolo" di Guillermo Del Toro: Una lettura post-razionalista. *Psicobiettivo*, 30: 155–168.

Metz, C. (1974) The imaginary signifier. In *The Imaginary Signifier. Psychoanalysis and the Cinema*. Bloomington: Indiana University Press, 1982.

Mulvey, L. (1975) Visual pleasure and narrative cinema. *Screen*, 16(3): 6–18.

Quinodoz, D. (1994) *Emotional Vertigo: Between Anxiety and Pleasure*. London: Routledge, 1997.

Rank, O. (1914) *The Double. A Psychoanalytic Study*. Chapel Hill: University of North Carolina Press, 1971.

Reich, W. (1933) *The Mass Psychology of Fascism*. New York: Furrier, Strays and Jerks, 1970.

Rentschler, E. (Ed.) (1990) *The Films of G. W. Pabst. An Extraterritorial Cinema*. New Brunswick, NJ: Rutgers University Press.

Ries, P. (1995) Popularise and/or be damned: Psychoanalysis and film at the crossroads in 1925. *International Journal of Psycho-Analysis*, 76: 759–791.

Rilke, R. M. (1922) *Sonnets to Orpheus*. Translated by C. F. MacIntyre. Los Angeles: University of California Press, 2001.

Rossellini, R. (1973) A discussion of Neo-Realism: Rossellini interviewed by Mario Verdone. In *Screen*, 14 (4): 69–78.

Rossellini, R., Roncoroni, S. and Amidei, S. (1973) *The War Trilogy of Roberto Rossellini.* New York: Grossman.

Sabbadini, A. (1988) The replacement child. *Contemporary Psychoanalysis*, 24: 528–547.

——— (1989) Boundaries of timelessness. Some thoughts about the temporal dimension of the psychoanalytic space. *International Journal of Psycho-Analysis*, 70: 305–313.

——— (1993) Bound to the mast: Reflections on analytic abstinence. *Unpublished.*

——— (1999) Tempo, narcisismo e creatività. *Psicoanalisi e Metodo*, 3: 49–62. Roma: Borla.

——— (2006) *Hable Con Ella:* The talking cure, from Freud to Almodóvar. In A. Sabbadini (Ed.), *Projected Shadows. Psychoanalytic Reflections on the Representation of Loss in European Cinema.* London: Routledge, 2007, pp. 65–72.

——— (2014) *Boundaries and Bridges. Perspectives on Time and Space in Psychoanalysis.* London: Karnac Books.

Sachs, H. (1926) *Psychoanalyse. Rätsel des Unbewußten.* Berlin: Lichtbildbühne.

Scorsese, M. (1999) Why *Vertigo* is truly great. *The Guardian*, Friday Review, 5 March 1999, p. 4.

——— (1980) Introduction to Michael Powell's *Peeping Tom.* British Broadcasting Corporation.

Searles, H. (1975) The patient as therapist to his analyst. In *Countertransference and Related Subjects.* New York: International Universities Press, 1979, pp. 380–459.

Segal, C. (1989) *Orpheus: The Myth of the Poet.* Baltimore: Johns Hopkins Univ. Press.

Sekoff, J. (1996) *Nineteen Nineteen*: The capture of souls. *Projections*, 10 (1): 42–49.

Sharff, S. (1997) *The Art of Looking in Hitchcock's* Rear Window. New York: Limelight Editions.

Shaw, G. B. (1913) *Pygmalion.* Harlow: Longman, 1995.

Shelley, M. W. (1818) *Frankenstein, or The Modern Prometheus.* London: Wordsworth, 1995.

Sklarew, B. (1999) Freud and film. *Journal of the American Psychoanalytic Association*, 47: 1239–1247.

Smith, P. J. (2000) *Desire. The Cinema of Pedro Almodovar* (2nd ed.). London: Verso.

Sophocles. *Oedipus, King of Thebes.* Translated by Gilbert Murray. In *Fifteen Greek Plays.* New York: Oxford University Press, 1943.

Spoto, D. (1976) *The Art of Alfred Hitchcock.* New York: Doubleday, 1979.

Sterba, R. (1940) Aggression in the rescue fantasy. *Psychoanalytic Quarterly*, 9: 505–508.

Stok, D. (Ed.) (1993) *Kieslowski on Kieslowski.* London: Faber & Faber.

Stoller, R. (1986) *Sexual Excitement. Dynamics of Erotic Life.* London: Maresfield Library.

Truffaut, F. (1983) *Hitchcock.* New York: Simon & Schuster, 1984.

Verhaege, P. (1998) *Love in a Time of Loneliness.* London: Rebus Press, 1999.

Webster's New World Dictionary of the American Language, College Edition. Cleveland and New York: The World Publishing Company, 1966.

Wilder, T. (1927) *The Bridge of San Luis Rey.* London: Longmans.

Wilson, S. (1980) *Salvador Dali.* London: Tate Gallery.

Winnicott, D. W. (1968) The squiggle game. In *Psycho-Analytic Explorations,* edited by C. Winnicott, C., R. Shepherd, R, and M. Davis. Cambridge, MA: Harvard University Press, 1989.

Wood, R. (1989) *Hitchcock's Films. Revisited.* London: Faber & Faber.

Zola, É. (1867) *Thérèse Raquin.* Transl. Robin Buss. London: Penguin, 2004.

Index

The letter *n* following a number indicates a note on that page. The letter *f* following a number denotes a figure.